ISBN 0 85429 411 2

A FOULIS Motoring Book

First published 1984

© **Haynes Publishing Group**

Published by:
Haynes Publishing Group
Sparkford, Yeovil,
Somerset BA22 7JJ

Distributed in USA by:
Haynes Publications Inc.
861 Lawrence Drive, Newbury Park, California 91320, USA

Editor: Mansur Darlington
Dust jacket design: Rowland Smith
Page layout: Anne Wildey
Dust jacket colour picture: A Rolls-Royce Corniche series II (Copyright Rolls-Royce Motors Limited 1984)
Colour photographs: Chris Harvey, Les Brazier and Mark Wilkins, and courtesy of Rolls-Royce Motors Ltd.
Road tests and test extracts: Courtesy of *Motor, Autosport* and *CAR*
Printed in England by: J.H.Haynes & Co. Ltd

Titles in the *Super Profile* series

Ariel Square Four (F388)
BMW R69 & R69S (F387)
BSA Bantam (F333)
Honda CB750 sohc (F351)
MV Agusta America (F344)
Norton Commando (F335)
Sunbeam S7 & S8 (F363)
Triumph Thunderbird (F353)
Triumph Trident (F352)

Austin-Healey 'Frogeye' Sprite (F343)
Ferrari 250GTO (F308)
Fiat X1/9 (F341)
Ford Cortina 1600E (F310)
Ford GT40 (F332)
Jaguar E-Type (F370)
Jaguar D-Type & XKSS (F371)
Jaguar Mk 2 Saloons (F307)
Jaguar SS90 & SS100 (F372)
Lancia Stratos (F340)
Lotus Elan (F330)
MGB (F305)
MG Midget & Austin-Healey Sprite (except 'Frogeye') (F344)
Morris Minor Series MM (F412)
Morris Minor & 1000 (ohv) (F331)
Porsche 911 Carrera (F311)
Rolls-Royce Corniche (F411)
Triumph Stag (F342)

B29 Superfortress (F339)
Boeing 707 (F356)
Harrier (F357)
Phantom II (F376)
Sea King (F377)
Super Etendard (F378)

Further titles in this series will be published at regular intervals. For information on new titles please contact your bookseller or write to the publisher.

FOREWORD

One of the chief attractions of the Rolls-Royce Corniche is that everything about it seems just right. Its concept as an exclusive version of the normal Rolls-Royce Silver Shadow, with an accent on the pleasurable aspects of driving, is not only thoroughly laudable but highly commercial even at a substantially greater price. It is hardly surprising either that the drop-head version has proved twice as popular as the fixed-head and continues in production today. There are few convertible cars available, let alone genuine four to five-seaters. There is the point also that air conditioning is fitted as standard, so that with the hood erect none of the comforts of a luxury saloon are lost. The Corniche was also introduced at a time when continuing development of the Silver Shadow had resulted in considerable improvements in straight-line stability and handling and sophistication of transmission operation. So every Corniche ever made is something of a classic. For the same reasons, it is impossible to isolate it from its place in the history of the Silver Shadow. This means that the story of the Corniche as we know it today is also the story of the Silver Shadow in its ultimate form as one of the most desirable Rolls-Royces ever made.

In compiling material for this book thanks are gratefully extended to *Motor* for permission to reproduce the Corniche Saloon road test, and to *Autosport* and *CAR* for permission to quote from road tests. We are also indebted to Rolls-Royce Motors Limited, in particular Ian Adcock, for courteous help.

Chris Harvey

HISTORY & EVOLUTION

There are sceptics who claim that the only real way to appreciate a Rolls-Royce is to ride in the back seat. The implication – one that rankled with Rolls-Royce – is that the cars are not so nice to drive. It was especially upsetting because they have always been car makers, above all others, that are anxious to please their clients and to give them unparalleled service and satisfaction. Nobody knows better than Rolls-Royce how many of their clients prefer to drive their cars themselves, rather than to be wafted along in a different, chauffeured, world. It was the philosophy of setting out to please the owner-driver that led to the introduction of the Corniche's first post-war predecessor, the S-series Continental.

These special-bodied Rolls-Royces were still being built at Mulliner Park Ward's coachworks at Willesden, North London, when the Corniche's most direct ancestor, the Silver Shadow, was announced in October 1965. The Silver Shadow had a pre-production development period of ten years, having been created to a brief of producing a carriage (or car) that was outwardly smaller than the last of the 'traditional' Rolls-Royces, the Silver Cloud, introduced in 1955, but even bigger inside. At the time, unitary construction, in which a car's chassis and body are combined as one unit, was in its infancy. But it was an effective solution to the problem of reducing the external proportions of the car without sacrificing the comfort of its occupants. Harry Grylls, chief engineer of the motor car division of Rolls-Royce, reckoned that with ten years for development, the new model should represent a significant advance over the Silver Cloud, which had reached the limits of its traditional construction with a chassis, and what amounted to a special coachbuilt body.

By its very nature, unitary construction reduced the possibilities of making truly individual any variants on the same theme in the way that a car with a chassis could be fitted with totally different bodywork from that used on similar chassis. So the Corniche, as the projected open version of the standard Silver Shadow saloon, became very important to Rolls-Royce as a way of showing that they could still make cars for the individual in an age when it was economic to make only cars with a strong element of conformity.

By using the body structure as a chassis, it was possible to make the car much lower, and a little narrower, without impinging upon the passengers' comfort. In the event, the Silver Shadow turned out to be 4.25 in lower, 3.75 in narrower, and 7.5 in shorter than the standard Silver Cloud, with overall dimensions of 4 ft 11.75 in in height, 5 ft 11 in in width, and 16 ft 11.5 in in length. The car's occupants actually gained from all this with a maximum width across the front seats of 4 ft 8.5 in and 4 ft 6 in in the back against the old standard of 4ft 5.5 in at the front and 4ft 5 in in the back. It is significant that the front compartment of the Silver Shadow gained the most from these manoeuvres, in keeping with the new car's appeal to a younger clientele, a far larger proportion of whom preferred to drive themselves. This policy was also essential in view of the importance of the Corniche-to-come.

Rolls-Royce also responded to the demands of an increasing American market by making the luggage boot – or trunk – much bigger with a maximum length of 4 ft 4 in, height of 1 ft 7 in, and width of 4 ft 11 in, against the Silver Cloud's maximum length in this department of 3 ft 10 in, height of 1 ft 3 in and width of 5 ft 1 in. The shape of the new boot also allowed the maximum height to be continued for a far greater length than had been allowed by the Silver Cloud's slim tail. With such gains in interior accommodation, the combination of the chassis and body to effect such a dramatic reduction in exterior size was supremely logical. The new, outwardly smaller, Rolls-Royce was much easier to handle in dense traffic, which showed no signs, in 1965, of ever getting any easier.

The Silver Shadow – Development

Rolls-Royce also considered that the adoption of unitary construction was desirable because it was so much more rigid than the old method. This meant that a modern, soft, suspension system could be used to give the best ride and handling characteristics. It was decided eventually to use independent rear suspension, to save space, rather than a de Dion arrangement, with its substantial linking tube. With either system, the final drive and propeller shaft remained virtually static, which meant that their housings encroached less on the space needed for the interior and luggage boot than if these components had needed room in which to move up and down. The main problems associated with the use of independent rear suspension and unitary construction were those of noise. A unitary body could act like a sounding box for any road-noise and especially for a solidly-mounted final drive and propeller shaft. Rolls-Royce were not too perturbed by these problems because they had ten years to iron them out and no particular restraint on the engineering budget to achieve this end. The ultimate solution, settled in the boardroom before development started in earnest, was to mount the suspension on sub-frames, front and rear, and to insulate these as effectively as possible from the body structure. Experience gained in mounting the exhaust system of the last of the Silver Clouds was used to good effect in this context.

The Silver Shadow's suspension sub-frames were attached to the body by flexible mountings spread wide apart for maximum stability. Vibrashock mountings like those used on the Silver Cloud III's exhaust system were adopted because they acted like variable-rate springs. This was because they were made from mesh that was compressed to such an extent that it offered low damping for small movements and a far higher degree for large movements because of internal friction in the wire mesh cushion.

The single-piece front sub-frame was mounted on four Vibrashocks, with a Panhard rod to limit its lateral movement in relation to the body; the rear sub-frame was more complex. It was made up of two cross-members, one for the final drive and one for the suspension. The first was firmly bolted to the final drive unit, then attached to the floorpan by four Vibrashocks, two vertical and two horizontal. The horizontal Vibrashocks were reinforced by a double-acting hydraulic damper and the cross-member itself attached to two tubular tie-bars by rubber mountings to counter any tendency to move sideways and promote rear-wheel steering. These tie-bars splayed outwards from the central mounting point on the body structure. The two cross-members

were linked by a deep steel torque arm rigidly bolted to the right side of the final drive casing with a rubber mounting at its far end.

The sub-frames were made from steel pressings with the front one carrying the engine and transmission on three rubber mountings. In this way, the power train was effectively insulated from the body structure by, first, its rubber mountings, and then by the sub-frame's Vibrashocks, which had been reinforced by coil springs.

The bodyshell, made up of steel pressings assembled at Cowley, near Oxford, by the Pressed Steel division of British Leyland, followed conventional lines with two bulkheads, front and rear, linked by box-section sills, inner wings and solid floors. The roof, outer wings, rear tonneau, luggage boot lip, and scuttle, contributed to its rigidity, which, at 10,800 feet per degree of twist for the 9 foot 11.5 inch wheelbase, was well up to standards established by other unitary-construction cars. Body panels which could be moved by hand, the doors, bonnet and luggage boot lid, were made from aluminium so that they were light to the touch. They also saved overall weight, of course.

The suspension itself followed conventional lines with wishbones at the front and the semi-trailing arms at the back. Coil-spring and Girling telescopic damper units were used as the suspension medium with a relatively soft setting for the most comfortable ride. The pivot axis of the upper arms of the front wishbones was inclined to the rear to give a measure of anti-dive reaction. The pivot points were also spread well apart with the front ones placed well forward to further reduce the downward force on the front of the car under braking.

The suspension was so soft, in fact, that it was found necessary to provide automatic self-levelling. This was achieved by making the coil spring mountings on the

bodyshell moveable by hydraulic means. This form of self-levelling did not influence the actual suspension of the car in the manner of the British Leyland Hydrolastic system or that of the Citroen cars where there was a constant fore-and-aft interaction, despite some parts being made to Citroen patents. The self-levelling system's function was to lower the top anchorage points of the springs as much as 3 inches at the back and 1 inch at the front when the weight of extra passengers or luggage was sufficient to force the body down towards the ground. Naturally the rear rams – which had to absorb more radical weight changes – did most of the work, but they did it very slowly while the car was in motion. They took from between 30 seconds and 1 minute to rise or fall 0.5 inch, the front rams working at only half that rate. When the car was stationary, with the gear selector in neutral, or a door was open, they worked at the rate of 0.5 inch per second. The slow working rate while the car was in motion was to ensure that they did not affect the normal suspension medium. The reason for this arrangement was that it is undesirable for the self-levelling system to try to correct roll when cornering or change the normal suspension's ability to soak up bumps. But there was no reason it should not compensate quickly for the weight of a passenger boarding or luggage being loaded into the boot when adjustment of the suspension height would not be having any effect on the car's handling. This duplex action in the self-levelling system was achieved by building a time-delay mechanism into the system that was over-ridden when the car was stationary with the gear selector in neutral or a door open.

This self-levelling system worked in conjunction with the hydraulic brakes through two independent circuits. Each was served by an identical single plunger pump set in the vee between the engine's cylinder banks and worked through a short push-rod from the camshaft. The pumps were linked to two spherical accumulators mounted low on the left side of the engine's crankcase. The accumulators had butyl separators, inflated with nitrogen to 1,000 psi. The hydraulic pumps pressurised these to a maximum of 2,500 psi, at which point pressure-regulating valves opened bypasses back to reservoirs in the accumulators. There were three height-control valves for the rams. One of them, at the front, was worked by an anti-roll bar incorporated in the suspension and the other two were operated by the rear suspension's trailing arms. The system was so carefully engineered that it worked without the sighs and groans often associated with similar systems on other cars. The accumulators not only stored a reserve supply of liquid under pressure, but they damped down sharp fluctuations in pressure.

One system — from the front pump — was responsible for 47 per cent of the total braking effort, which was divided 31 per cent to the front and 16 per cent to the rear. The other provided 31 per cent of the total effort to the front brakes alone and fed the self-levelling system. Disc brakes were fitted all round with two independent twin-cylinder calipers at the front and a single four-cylinder caliper on each rear brake. One pair of cylinders on each rear caliper was served by a third, conventional, hydraulic system with a master cylinder. These made up the remaining 22 per cent of the total braking effort. Its main purpose was to provide a degree of feeling for the driver through the brake pedal. It was not fitted with a servo, which would have masked any such feeling. Its master cylinder contained a pressure-limiting valve to reduce any likelihood of the rear wheels locking under braking.

Loss of pressure in a braking circuit was indicated by a tell-tale lamp on the instrument panel, and

any failure did not affect the other two hydraulic systems. A fourth braking system was provided by a mechanical handbrake working on the pistons served by the third system's master cylinder. The brakes' friction pads were fitted with sensors that lit a warning lamp on the instrument panel when they were worn to such an extent that they needed replacement. It had been decided to fit these disc brakes to all four wheels rather than to continue with the Silver Cloud's drum brakes — which had been proven to be perfectly adequate — so that the latest advances in braking technology could be considered for the Silver Shadow, as it was thought that drum brakes had reached the limit of their development. Drum brakes had also been shown to be inadequate on lesser cars than a Silver Cloud, so there was a sound marketing reason for changing to discs which everybody considered to be superior even if they were not.

The Silver Shadow was fitted with American Saginaw recirculating ball steering gear with a constant ratio of 19.3:1, which gave 4.25 turns lock-to-lock on a new, two-spoke, 17-inch diameter steering wheel. Although the ratio was slightly higher than that of the Silver Cloud, it still retained the Rolls-Royce ideal of the 'sneeze' factor where slight movements when concentration might be impaired would not be enough to move the car off course. The power assistance was still supplied by a Hobourn-Eaton pump as in the Silver Cloud, but compared with the earlier car, the steering load was reduced still further, as was the turning circle to 38 feet. The steering column was positioned out of line with the input shaft and connected to it by a short, jointed, section so that any impact shocks from an accident would not be fed up the column. The couplings were of rubber at the top and ball and trunnion at the bottom. A lever-arm hydraulic damper was incorporated in the steering idler. The steering

lever on the pump's output shaft was connected to the idler by a cross-beam. Two ball joints near the centre of this beam were coupled to steering arms ahead of the stub axles by track rods.

The front suspension's geometry was so arranged that it had a 68 per cent anti-dive factor with a front wheel range of movement of 4 inches on bump and rebound; the back, with its constant velocity inboard universal joints and Hooke-type outer joints, provided complete freedom of lift under braking with 3.5 in of wheel movement on bump and 5.5 in on rebound.

Five-stud steel wheels of 15 in diameter and 6 in width were used with 8.45–15 in low-profile cross-ply tyres. Radial-ply tyres were not fitted at first because they were considered too noisy for a Rolls-Royce.

But they were fitted to the Corniche from its introduction in March 1971 with some suspension changes because handling was of paramount importance with the more sporting car. Radial-ply tyres in the section that Rolls-Royce needed for cars based on the Silver Shadow had also become readily-available by then. The front and rear tracks of the Silver Shadow were the same at 4 ft 9.5 in, with a ground clearance, laden, of 6.5 in. When the car was at rest, it simply sat on its springs with the self-levelling rams unpressurised. They then came into operation, when the engine was running, to maintain the ride height. The Silver Shadow's roll centre was calculated to be 4 ins above ground level in this condition, near to the parallel roll axis.

The engine and transmission of the Silver Shadow were similar to those fitted to the Silver Cloud, the engine's introduction dating from September 1959. It was an all-aluminium vee-eight, the configuration having been selected as the best available for installation in the more restricted engine bays of modern cars. With a vast experience of engine design and building, Rolls-Royce were confident that they could contain the mechanical noise that would not be as well damped by aluminium as it would have been using the more conventional cast iron. Aluminium for the cylinder heads and block not only made the unit lighter, but dispersed better the heat generated.

A variety of methods were used to keep down the engine's width – often a problem with an engine of vee formation. Although the angle of the bores was at a conventional 90 degrees, which kept down the height, the stroke was also relatively short, which kept down the width and allowed the engine to rev more freely. These relatively large cylinder bores allowed the use of in-line valves, in conjunction with an efficient wedge-shaped combustion chamber. At the same time, each valve could be given an individual port with ample room for coolant passages. The cylinder heads were interchangeable, and the connecting rods ran alongside each other, which meant that the two banks of cylinders were offset. The crankshaft ran in five main bearings of 2.5 in diameter with a single helical gear at the front driving the camshaft. The gear was forged from aluminium, which Rolls-Royce had found could be made to last longer than steel, and imposed less stress on the shaft. This also meant that it ran much quieter, with high-pitched vibrations eliminated by flutes cast in the centre. Such a system was quieter than a chain drive, as were the hydraulic tappets developed by Chrysler in America. Needless to say, great care was taken in the assembly of this engine, and to giving it a clean and tidy appearance. It had a capacity of 6.2 litres when it was first used in the Silver Shadow, increased in 1970 to 6,750 cc to provide more torque so that it could combat the addition of American emission equipment. This capacity increase was achieved by lengthening the

stroke by 7.7 mm to 99.1 mm, the bores remaining unchanged at 104.1 mm. This engine's power was increased by 10 per cent to around 240 hp – although Rolls-Royce would not be drawn into a horsepower race by stating its output – by removing the US Federal anti-pollution equipment, fitting Lucas OPUS electronic ignition, retiming the camshaft to give more efficient breathing at the top end of the range (at the expense of heavier fuel consumption), increasing the bore of the exhaust system from 2 in to 2.225 in, and fitting a more efficient air cleaner. These last two changes carried the penalties of slightly more noise. But the changes increased the performance and made the car feel more sporting.

Initially, the Silver Shadow had a fluid coupling and a four-speed automatic gearbox like that of the Silver Cloud, but this had given way to a General Motors' Hydramatic, which, although it had only three speeds, was, when linked to the normal torque converter, far smoother in operation. This gearbox had been refined in America to such an extent that Rolls-Royce did not feel that it was necessary to build it themselves; they simply fitted it as supplied, confident that their rigorous tests would reveal any deficiencies in manufacture. A simple, two-piece, propeller shaft with a resonance damper at the rear end linked the gearbox to the hypoid final drive, which had a ratio of 3.08:1. This gave 26.2 mph for 1000 rpm in top gear.

Although Rolls-Royce could not justify the enormous cost and space occupied by the giant presses needed to produce unitary bodyshells – such investment could only be met by an organisation as big as Pressed Steel, producing hundreds of thousands of bodies a year, rather than the anticipated 2,000 or so Rolls and Bentley shells – they went to a great deal of trouble to finish the body properly.

Inadequately-finished unitary construction shells, where the amount and application of paint and corrosion-proofing matter is controlled by a strict budget, are particularly prone to rust, especially in countries where salt is commonly used on the roads to combat ice and snow. Rolls-Royce countered this problem by insisting on the use of expensive heavy-gauge zinc-coated steel in their shells in areas that were particularly prone to corrosion in normal cases. In addition, all spot-welded areas were painted with zinc primer before assembly. Following delivery from Pressed Steel, the bodyshells were cleaned and checked for imperfections.

Standard underbody panels and floorpans were then assembled with new door posts and outer panels to take the two-door bodywork which distinguished early coachbuilt examples of the Silver Shadow, and the Corniche which followed. From the windscreen forward, the early coachbuilt cars, introduced in March 1966, were the same as the standard Silver Shadow saloon, although they differed considerably behind that. A new roof was fitted with different rear wings, which were styled with a rounded theme at waistline level above the rear wheel arches. New, far wider, doors were made from aluminium, enabling the rear seats to be reached when either front seat was folded forward. Once completed, these shells were transported to Crewe, where, like the saloon, the shell underwent a six-stage process of dipping and spraying in which the surface of the metal acquired a zinc-like quality which inhibited corrosion and improved paint adhesion. Then the shells were washed with distilled-water and dried in an oven before being immersed in primer. This was baked before a thorough inspection for imperfections. The body joints were then sealed with a flexible plastic compound and two layers of surface primer applied by hand with a stoving process after each coat. It was at that point that the underseal was applied. In common with manufacturers such as Porsche — renowned for their attempts to stave off corrosion — Rolls-Royce used a great deal of underseal, its total weight in the Silver Shadow amounting to 70 lb. The bodyshells were then rubbed down by hand and more primer applied as a sealer. More rubbing down by hand followed before another thorough inspection. These 'thorough inspections' were more like formal military parades than the numerous ordinary inspections the shell received during the course of its preparation.

Two coats of the final colour were then applied to the body and stoved before they were flatted by hand. Again, a thorough inspection followed before the final two coats of paint and yet another inspection prior to polishing. Most of the car's chrome-work still had to be fitted at this stage and to avoid potential damage to the chrome, the cars were road tested in this condition on slave wheels.

After the very thorough road test, the cars were returned to the paint shop for the underseal to be made good and the entire underside to be sprayed with bituminous material, plus yet another thorough inspection before final assembly and the grand inspection.

The interior construction followed no less stringent routines, being made in the time-honoured Rolls-Royce manner. The veneers were as good as those in any other Rolls-Royce and so was the quality of the leather, cloth and carpets. Although the Silver Shadow had an extra couple of inches of shoulder room over that of the Silver Cloud, it was still essentially a four-seater. Three people could sit abreast in the back seat, but not in the standard of comfort expected in a Rolls-Royce. But, for four people, two in the front and two in the back, everything was as comfortable as before, with even more attention to detail. The front

seats could be moved electrically in eight different directions, by a tiny horizontal lever like the joy-stick in an aircraft. Small wedge-shaped footrests were fitted for back-seat passengers, who also had two folding tables in the backs of the front seats, reading lamps, general lamps, map pockets and vanity mirrors. Folding central armrests were fitted front and back with ashtrays and lighters.

Power for the four-headlamp lighting system and numerous electrical systems within the car was supplied by a negative earth 12-volt battery charged by a 35-amp dynamo. Cars fitted with air conditioning had an optional 40-amp alternator as standard. Many more printed circuits were used in the electrical system than before, with multi-pin sockets where necessary to ease maintenance. The use of electrical assistance for the driver and passengers was even more extensive than before. The radio aerial was now raised and lowered electrically, the fuel filler trap door could be released from the driver's seat, and the heated rear window element was controlled by a thermostat. The parking lamp selector switch enabled either left-hand, or right-hand parking lights to be illuminated individually, and was contained in circuit with the starter, which could not be operated if only the parking lamps were on. When the main lighting switch was pulled out, with everything else off, a small lamp lit up above the ignition keyhole.

Warning lamps were fitted in a group: two reds for the brake accumulators; one green for low fuel level and one amber to show that the handbrake was still on or that one stoplamp bulb had failed. The operation of these warning lamps could be tested by switching on the ignition and pressing the oil-level indicator on the petrol gauge; all four warning lamps then lit up if they were working properly. A tell-tale switch was fitted above the rear view mirror to operate all four

indicators at once as a hazard warning when the car was stationary. Red warning lamps were fitted to show that a door was open and the battery had an auxiliary or charging socket. The fusebox was contained in a tray beneath the fascia.

Air conditioning was listed as an option on all Silver Shadows except those bound for the United States and Canada, which had it as standard. The air intake for this system was just in front of the windscreen with two fresh air pick-ups ducted from the front of the car to outlets each side of the scuttle and through the fascia. There were independent fans for left and right-hand side air flows and provision for a division of the air flow between high and low levels so that air of differing temperatures could be selected for head and feet. The lay-out of the refrigeration system in the air conditioning had been revised with the main components behind the fascia of the Silver Shadow. The instrument panel was also different from that of the Silver Cloud in that the dials were grouped in front of the driver.

Rolls-Royce continued their policy of development and improvement of their cars by introducing a convertible in September 1967. It had been relatively easy to build a drop-head coupé on previous Rolls-Royces because of the rigidity afforded by their massive chassis. The new unitary shell proved strong, but only sufficiently rigid for it to be used without a stressed steel roof when gussets and strengthening plates were welded in the area of the sills and scuttle. This also meant that there was no possibility of a four-door version of the drop-head coupé because the extra rigidity afforded by the forward extension of the rear wings on the two-door was essential. A far stronger rear door post was also fitted and the total extra weight of the convertible amounted to nearly 200 lb when the hood-lifting mechanism and complicated hood frame and fabric were weighed against the shells with a steel roof. Assembly of the drop-head coupé's bodyshell followed the same procedure as that of the fixed-head coupé. Its trim was also similar, except that different window frames were fitted so that a 'frameless' appearance could be presented when the hood (or top as it was called in America) was furled. Such was the bulk of the folding hood and its electric lifting mechanism (like that of the Silver Cloud III) that there was no room to fit air conditioning equipment – not that it would have been certain to have operated properly in a soft-topped car. The interiors of these special Silver Shadows, the fixed-head and the drop-head – which was called a convertible in America – followed the lines of the standard saloon.

In keeping with modern trends, the Silver Shadow's steering ratio was reduced to 3.7 turns from lock to lock in 1969 and all cars, except convertibles and those for the US and Canada, were fitted with a stiffer front anti-roll bar and a rear anti-roll bar at the same time. These changes in the suspension had the dual effect of making the ride a little stiffer. It was felt at the time that the North American market was not yet ready for a change in their 'boulevard' ride, and the convertible's shell was not quite stiff enough to accept uprated suspension. Greater leverage was provided for the hand brake and the radiator cooling fan was fitted with a viscous coupling to reduce the amount of power loss when driving it at high speeds. Thicker battery cables were adopted to improve their durability and brake bleeding was made easier by new valves in the hydraulic system. In addition, many cars were fitted with Avon cross-ply tyres to improve traction and wet-road grip. But the Silver Shadows did not get radial-ply tyres yet. They were to be introduced on the Corniche. In the meantime, all cars received a restyled interior that met US

Federal safety standards. This included a collapsible steering column, head restraints, and an instrument panel where much energy-absorbing material had been built in for protection in the event of an accident. The windscreen surround, the centre console, doors and handles, were all modified, and on the North American models only, the backs of the front seats were redesigned to eliminate the folding tables. These cars also received new clearance lights on their body sides and larger indicator lights. Manifold air injection equipment was fitted to US models, which reduced exhaust emissions at the expense of some power. The front ride height control was removed from all cars because it hardly ever came into operation.

The optional air conditioning, with alternator, was made standard in November 1969, because most customers ordered their cars with it in any case and people who did not order it showed no disinclination to buy a Rolls-Royce that cost a little more because of its fitting as standard. This meant there had to be some re-organisation of the belts at the front of the engine to take the refrigerator pump. Higher-geared steering was introduced at the same time as part of the gradual process of making the Silver Shadow more of a driver's car. Rolls-Royce were of the opinion that they should not raise the steering ratio too rapidly because owners – many of whom bought a new car every year – might complain of a dramatic change in its feeling. The oil pump was also improved and the rear cross-member stiffened at the same time as a result of comments by the development engineers who spent much time testing the cars. Side marker lamps incorporating reflectors were fitted to all cars from January 1970, with the new 6.7 litre engine in July.

Soon after, in September, more changes were evident. The electrical system was modified to give centralised door locking – and

unlocking – and the gear change mechanism altered so that it automatically locked itself into Park, regardless of the position of the gearlever, when the ignition key was removed. The convenience of the centralised door locking was obvious; and the inconvenience to potential thieves of a transmission locked into Park when the gearlever was in another position could be imagined. A remote control exterior mirror was offered as an option; as was a tape player. Four radio speakers were fitted as standard and the electric seat adjustment was improved.

The Corniche series I

It was in this form that the Silver Shadow was used as a basis for the Corniche with the more powerful 6.7-litre engine, a stiffer bodyshell, revised front suspension to accept radial-ply tyres, ventilated disc brakes, a new 'sporting' fascia, and a more aggressive radiator shell.

The object of switching to radial-ply tyres was to improve the handling and traction. One of the reasons for the delay in fitting them – many cars had been using them for 10 years or more and the French Citroens for 20 years – was that they had only just become available in the same section as the cross-ply tyres used on the Silver Shadow. In order to insulate the car's occupants from the thumping and vibration that could be set up by the stiffer radial-ply tyres, Rolls-Royce made the front suspension more compliant. This entailed fitting new Metalastik sub-frame mountings in place of the Vibrashocks. These new rubber mountings, which were similar to those used on the Jaguar XJ6 (which was noted for its silent ride and superb handling on large, fat, radial-ply tyres), allowed more movement fore and aft in the suspension, but were more rigid laterally. This obviated the need for the Panhard rod. The suspension geometry was revised at the same time to give a higher roll centre, which meant changing virtually all the suspension parts in detail. The forged upper wishbones were replaced by fabricated ones, which were triangulated in such a way that they fed shocks generated by the road surface into the Metalastik mountings. The front track was increased from 57.5 in to 59.4 in. A useful by-product of the new suspension, which dictated the use of radial-ply tyres, was that the steering was made more responsive. US cars, which had previously been fitted with a thinner anti-roll bar, now had the same as used elsewhere, because there was no longer the same demand in North America for a boulevard ride. Customers, who had been looking with greater interest at the Mercedes range, were showing a preference for a more sporting feeling to the Silver Shadow and Corniche.

The suspension changes, in conjunction with radial-ply tyres, improved the Corniche's handling, and the new brakes provided an extra safety margin against the possibility of fade induced by the higher performance. Their ventilation was assisted by fitting more sporting pierced wheels with stainless steel trims to a new pattern.

To give the car a slightly more aggressive appearance, the new radiator shell was also raked forward three degrees. A sporting touch was given to the interior by fitting a tachometer and a 15-in wood-rim steering wheel that had the dual advantage of making the steering feel higher-geared. This did not prove to be too popular with customers, however, and was soon replaced with a 16-in plastic-rimmed wheel in August 1971, with a rise in the steering ratio to 3.5 turns from lock to lock.

Air conditioning was fitted as standard to the Corniche, the problems of installation and operation having been overcome in the drop-head coupé. Other items,

which had been optional extras on the Silver Shadow, such as the speed control, were fitted as standard to the Corniche. In this form, the Corniche took over completely from the earlier coachbuilt coupés, and commanded a list price of around 33 per cent more than the standard Silver Shadow and 25 per cent more than the long-wheelbase saloon built by the same methods. These figures were more than doubled at auction, such was the demand, and the waiting list stretched to four years for a new customer. One of the first journalists to try the new Corniche convertible was John Bolster, who reported in *Autosport* in March 1971:

'The car cruises with restful ease at up to 110 mph, and will reach a genuine 120 mph very quickly. I did not try beyond 120 mph as the rev counter was then just entering the red section, but the sound level did not differ from that at 30 mph. The rev-counter is an essential piece of equipment as the more powerful engine can achieve injudicious speeds so easily; an ignition cut-out would be a worthwhile addition, which shows how racing practice can be usefully employed on the most luxurious of cars.

'In spite of the great weight of such a car, it can be handled in a truly sporting fashion. It hangs on splendidly on fast curves, only the sound of the tyres betraying what is

afoot. On sharper corners, the degree of understeer never becomes excessive, and the independent rear suspension *almost* prevents wheelspin at the traffic-lights grand prix. The steering is so light that it might seem disconcerting at first to one unaccustomed to the car, but this is a matter of practice. As would be expected, the big machine is rock steady in side winds.

'The brakes are really silent at all times, controlling the weight with ease. Bolster recorded a maximum speed of 120 mph but did not have time to take acceleration or fuel consumption figures. *Autocar* had more time for a complete assessment when they tested a 1973-model fixed-head Corniche in April 1974. Their maximum speed was 120 mph, with acceleration figures of 0 – 60 mph in just under 10 seconds, and a standing-start quarter mile of just over 17 seconds; a substantial improvement on the Silver Shadow and impressive, by anyone's standards, for a two ton car.

Typical fuel consumption was 13 mpg, though this could easily fall to less than 10 mpg in heavy traffic, or during fast cruising, such as might be indulged in on continental excursions. Quite rightly, with a fuel tank capacity of only 24 gallons, the practical range was considered poor at little over 200 miles.

Autocar were impressed with how much progress had been made by that time with the suspension and noted how the balance between ride and handling had become a much better compromise. The steering response had been made faster and although understeer was still predominant, with power on the Corniche had much nearer neutral characteristics than the Silver Shadow previously tested.

At the same time as the Silver Shadows were being updated to accept the Corniche front suspension and brakes in August 1973, the rectangular air inlets

beneath the headlights were found to be unnecessary. So they were deleted and quartz halogen foglights were fitted as standard above the front bumper. The exhaust system was improved and now had a horizontal end rather than the earlier down-sloping tail pipe. Cars bound for North America were fitted with energy-absorbing bumpers to comply with new safety laws. They also received a foot parking brake to meet popular demand.

The development of new and improved radial-ply tyres resulted in Rolls-Royce's fitting HR70-HR15 low-profile rubberware in April 1974. The suspension geometry was modified to suit these tyres, which led to a dramatic change in the appearance of the car because the wheelarches had to be flared to cover them. This was partly because the front track was increased by 0.5 in to 5 ft and the rear track by 2.875 in to 4 ft 11.023 in. This meant that the car was now 5 ft 11.7 at its widest point, across the flared arches.

Motor found the suspension changes to their liking when they tested a fixed-head Corniche in October 1975. They said of the handling:

'The understeer which characterised previous Rolls-Royce cars, and made them rather tiresome to drive along a twisting road, is much less apparent. Some initial understeer still exists when turning into a corner but it is by no means excessive and helps to convey a great feeling of security'.

Motor were not so happy with the back-seat access, however, and noted that it was possible to stow only 12.7 cu ft of luggate in the boot, against 14.5 cu ft for the Silver Shadow, because of the room taken by the air-conditioning system. They also detected some bodyshake over rough roads with the big new tyres, and suggested a revised seat belt mounting, saying:

'The Corniche has very thin pillars behind the doors, too thin for mounting sufficiently strong seat

belt anchorages. Rolls-Royce have therefore mounted the top mount on the waistline, a position which means the belt is intolerably difficult to find and put on, and infuriatingly prone to slipping off when in use. A roof mount used in conjunction with a slave arm which ensures that the diagonal doesn't cut across your neck (as on the new Open Manta) would be far better.'

The Corniche Series II

Development continued to such an extent during 1976 that the next round of changes led to Rolls-Royce's adopting a series II designation for the Silver Shadows and the Corniche. These changes included some items which had been pioneered in 1975 on the expensive coachbuilt Camargue fixed-head coupé, which used the Corniche as a basis. There was a new form of steering, improvements to the suspension and aerodynamics, minor changes to the engine, a new air conditioning system and a revised instrument panel. The Silver Shadow II, and Corniche series II, introduced in February 1977, could be readily identified by the North American-style polyurethane-faced bumpers. These were the same as those on the earlier US cars, except that they were not mounted on energy-absorbing struts for any other market.

The new steering, by Burman power-assisted rack and pinion, was similar to that used on British Leyland's Rover 3500. It certainly countered the mounting criticism of the lack of feeling in the Silver Shadow and Corniche's steering and involved a number of other changes. The front suspension geometry was revised to give more camber. A change which meant that the wheels stayed in a more upright position while cornering. This also helped to make the steering feel more responsive and reduced tyre wear. The rear anti-roll

bar was reduced in diameter in keeping with the front suspension settings. One of the hydraulic system's accumulators had to be moved from the left side of the engine to the right to make room for the new steering gear. The exhaust manifolds also had to be changed. Instead of having front-end offtakes, they now had central downpipes, bridged by a small balance pipe.

In the interests of fuel economy and emission control, 1.875-in SU HIF7 carburettors were fitted and sealed against unauthorised adjustment. They operated successfully on a far weaker mixture when idling than the earlier 2 in instruments, and reflected how the energy crisis of 1974 had reached even Corniche owners. A cartridge oil filter replaced the earlier felt one at the same time.

Engines using a weaker mixture run hotter, so new radiator cooling fans were fitted. These took the form of smaller, but more efficient, seven-bladed plastic fans in place of the earlier single fan. The main fan was supported by a new electric fan ahead of the radiator matrix, which was set to cut in at 105°C (302°F). These new fans also saved power and reduced the noise which could be heard from outside the car. A 75-amp alternator was fitted to cope with the extra load on the electrical system.

A new wash-and-wipe system for the headlamps contributed to this. The frontal appearance of the Corniche and Silver Shadow was also affected by the adoption of an air dam to further improve straight-line stability by reducing front-end lift, particularly in gusty winds. This was developed as a result of experience with the Camargue. The radiator shell of the series II was made 0.47 in deeper at the same time and the overall length of the car increased to 17 ft 0.5 in by the new bumpers. The foglights were now mounted under the front bumper ahead of the air dam. An internally adjustable mirror on the driver's door was fitted to all cars to meet EEC regulations.

The new air conditioning, developed on the Camargue, provided completely independent temperature control at both upper and lower levels. One of the objects of its design was that it should be simple to operate and not need adjustment to meet changes in the temperature outside the car, or to cope with heat from the sun on the windows. The heating and refrigeration systems were similar to those of the earlier Corniche but its sensors and controls were new. The upper system worked through the windscreen demister vents, two outlets for the occupants of the front seats and a central outlet for the rear-seat passengers. The lower system had vents near the floor in the front and back. Fans on the side of the scuttle boosted the airflow when necessary. Two selectors were fitted to control upper and lower temperatures. A third selector had five positions: low, to give automatic temperature control with the fans at their slowest speed; high for the fans at their highest speed; defrost for the full heat output to be directed at the inside of the windscreen; off; and auto, at which a chosen temperature could be maintained regardless of what was going on outside the car.

The air conditioning was controlled by sensors inside and outside the car. The upper system used three, one under the rear bumper to monitor ambient temperature, one on the interior cantrail for the top-half temperature, and one on the top roll for solar heat. The lower system had an outside sensor under the rear bumper and another at knee height ahead of the front passenger's seat. The rear window demister was operated the sensors which were linked to a computer which operated flaps on the air vents and blended hot and cold air from the system. The incoming air was dehumidified to stop the windows misting up. Used

air was expelled through vents in the rear parcel shelf and let out through the luggage boot. An oil pressure switch stopped the air conditioning from being used while the engine was not running, to avoid flattening the battery. The fans did not work – except on defrost – until the heated water had reached 44°C (111°F) to avoid blasting the occupants with cold air unless it was desired to reduce the temperature inside the car. A 13-second delay was built into the operation of the fans so that they did not restart with humid air trapped in the vents, which might cause the windows to mist. The lower air system was also shut off while the engine was warming up in deference to the occupants' feet. This new system was able to provide cooler air than before, with a temperature range of between 16°C (60°F) and 33°C (90°F). An outside ambient temperature and ice warning gauge for the instrument panel was incorporated in this system.

Revisions to the panel included a new four-in-one instrument for fuel, oil pressure, the electrical system's charging rate, and engine coolant temperature. An electronic speedometer – still reading up to 999,999 miles – was fitted to reduce the possibility of noise from the driving cable of a conventional instrument.

A new speed control was fitted to the end of the gearlever and the control switches were made easier to read in the dark. A new, smaller, 15.25-in steering wheel had its spokes repositioned to make it easier to read the instruments and warning lights. The fusebox was also repositioned in a more accessible spot below the passenger's glove compartment. The air conditioning controls were carried on a revised centre console.

In accordance with the Rolls-Royce policy of introducing major new mechanical components first in the two-door models, they fitted the Corniche (and Camargue) with a revised rear suspension during

1979. This was intended for the latest saloon, the Silver Spirit, which was to be introduced in 1980. Rolls-Royce's targets were an improvement in ride and handling and a reduction in road noise and body roll, points which had raised criticism from customers as well as the specialist motoring Press. With the new suspension, the trailing arms were inclined closer together. The resultant revision in geometry meant that the wheels remained more upright in their travel, in a similar manner to the changes to the front suspension geometry in 1977. This reduced tyre scrub when cornering. At the same time, the roll centre was raised by 2 in which reduced body roll and further improved the handling. The leading cross-member was tied to the rear one by a series of stiff links to make the entire suspension mounting one rigid assembly. These new links allowed a little fore and aft movement but virtually no lateral movement, which meant that the rear wheels were better controlled and road noise reduced. New hydropneumatic struts, inspired by those fitted to Citroen's GS and CX saloons, were fitted to improve the ride. Their pick-up points were 4 in behind the rear wheel centre line. These struts had a better rising rate capability, so they could be set more softly. This meant that they carried a load better and were more compatible with the existing self-levelling system. Rolls-Royce kept this new suspension as secret as possible, but Mel Nichols, then editor of *CAR* magazine, was lucky enough to be able to test a Corniche drop-head with the new suspension just as the Silver Spirit was introduced. He reported in the issue of *CAR* magazine of October 1980:

'From the instant you begin driving this revised Corniche you notice that it has benefited a great deal from the presence of the new suspension, and from other refinement work. The steering, which used to be so awful before

Rolls switched to rack and pinion, is now beautiful. Initially, the rack wasn't all that impressive, but constant tuning has meant that now it's a pleasure to touch the big, thin-rimmed wheel and to turn it; the weighting is excellent and the smoothness of the motion quite delicious. And the response of the car to the steering is now laudable. Then you notice that, at low speeds over knobbly city streets, the Corniche is riding very smoothly and quietly; the old traces of lumpiness and tyre patter have been all but eliminated. Moreover, the car feels more stable and better-controlled, and is thus even easier to whip through city streets. The Corniche has a surprisingly tight turning circle, is conveniently narrow for its length and high enough to give the driver very good vision in traffic. While the ultimate performance is good rather than breathtaking the bagfuls of torque from the engine, multiplied by the big GM automatic transmission, mean that there is real oomph away from standstill. Thus in town the Corniche is a handy car, a marvellous car – it blends its manoeuvrability and response with quietness and real luxury so that the driver and his passengers are effectively removed from the hubbub around them. It doesn't seem to matter whether the top is up or down. And the condition is real: it isn't just that you're riding behind that famous mascot.

'While the Corniche benefits discernibly from its update, its body's lack of rigidity and the noise allowed by the cloth roof mean that it obviously isn't the ultimate showpiece for the new rear suspension. That will require the Silver Spirit itself. In the Corniche, the suspension itself copes very well with poor surfaces, but there are often bump-created tremors right through the Corniche's vast, open body. You can feel them in the seat, at the wheel rim and see them at the scuttle. They're not severe, but they're there; not even Rolls-Royce can overcome the inherent difficulties in making a large open car that doesn't even have the structural assistance of a rollover bar. You learn to live with these tremors.

'You must also learn to live with the Corniche when it rains. It is a quick-handling car in that, with any sort of power applied, it corners neutrally with an increasing bias, as the prodigious weight takes over with speed, towards roll oversteer. In other words, the back comes round very quickly. In the wet, it will come around and let go with very little provocation. So you learn to use only the slightest trace of power when you're cornering if you wish to avoid what many might regard as the unseemly sight of a Corniche going very sideways. All this happens at very modest speeds: 20 mph on a South Circular road right-hander, for instance. Although there is *more* roadholding than before, the level in the dry isn't very high either. There's just too much weight to contend with and building in understeer would be no answer at all ...

'Driving within its limits is, however, a smooth and pleasant experience most of the time because the steering is so smooth and accurate and the body motion is (then) so well-controlled ...

'But what is so nice about the car is the way things feel – the steering, the brakes, all the minor controls, the door locks, the action of the bonnet when you lift it. Rolls-Royce have made the quality of the movement of such things an art form, so beautiful to the touch that a Rolls-Royce is the most sensuous car there is ... that, of course, is the Rolls-Royce secret.'

SPECIFICATION

Type	Rolls-Royce Corniche series I and II, Bentley Corniche series I and II
Number built (to December 1983) approx	Rolls-Royce Corniche convertible 2,500
	Bentley Corniche convertible 100
	Rolls-Royce Corniche saloon 1,300
	Bentley Corniche saloon 100
Engine	(UK) V8, aluminium alloy cylinder blocks and heads, 6,750 cc, 411.7 cu in, 104.1 mm bore, 99.1 mm stroke, two 2 in SU carburettors, Lucas OPUS electronic ignition, power approx 240 bph. (US) As UK except re-timed camshaft, US Federal-specification emission equipment, power approx 225 bhp. (series II) twin 1.875 in SU H1F7 carburettors.
Transmission	Torque converter and three-speed GM Hydramatic box, ratios 1.0, 1.5, 2.5. Hypoid bevel final drive, ratio 3.08:1.
Chassis	Sheet steel monocoque, combined body/chassis unit. Wheelbase 9ft 11.5in, track (series I), front and rear, 4ft 9.5in; from April 1974, front 5ft 0in, rear 4ft 11in.
Suspension	(series I) front, independent wishbones and coil springs, anti-roll bar; rear, independent, trailing arms, coil springs, anti-roll bar, hydraulic height control rams; from 1979, hydropneumatic struts at rear.
Steering	(series I) Saginaw recirculating ball, ratio 19.3:1; 17.5:1 from August 1971. (series II) Burman rack and pinion.
Brakes	11 in disc all round, three-stage hydraulic operation.
Wheels and tyres	(series I) 15 in x 6 in ventilated disc, 205-15 in radial-ply tyres; from April 1974 HR70-HR15 radial-ply tyres.
Bodywork	Two-door drophead or fixed-head; from March 1980, drophead only.
Dimensions	(series I) Overall length 16ft 11.5in, width 5ft 11in, height 4ft 11.75in, from April 1974 width 5ft 11.7in; (series II) length 17ft 0.5in, unladen weight (saloon) 4,978 lb (convertible) 5,124lb.
Performance	120mph maximum, 0-60 mph 9.6 sec, standing start quarter mile 17.1 sec, fuel consumption 12 mpg.

MOTOR week ending October 4 1975

ROAD TEST

ROLLS-ROYCE CORNICHE

FOR : construction and finish ; engine noise ; brakes ; automatic transmission ; comfort ; smoothness ; equipment

AGAINST : price, fuel consumption ; road noise ; seat belts ; seat shape ; getting in the back

Rolls-Royce. A very special name. One that conjures up visions of opulence, sophistication, luxury and hedonism, as well as technical excellence. As a symbol of success, you can aspire to nothing higher.

But no company can continue to live on its reputation alone. It must continually revise, refine and update its products to keep ahead of ever-rising standards. This is one of the secrets of Rolls-Royce's success, for their policy is one of steady improvement. The Silver Shadows and Corniches of today may look much the same as they did on introduction but under the skin there are many changes; wide, low profile radial-ply tyres; revised suspension and steering; and lots of electrical revisions including items such as a central locking/unlocking system, intermittent wiper action and delayed courtesy light mechanism.

And there's no disputing Rolls-Royce's success. The present company, called Rolls-Royce Motors Ltd, has traded very profitably since its formation in March 1971 from the automotive activities of the bankrupt Rolls-Royce Ltd. Between 1971 and 1974 turnover increased from £38.35m to £58.39m with a corresponding improvement in pre-tax profits (£6.3m instead of £3.8m). For the past three years running, Rolls-Royce have exceeded all previous sales records. Unlike other up-market companies, they haven't been hit very hard by the fuel crisis. All that's happened is that the waiting list for Rolls-Royce models is much shorter than once it was. It now takes about one year to receive delivery of a Corniche built to your specification, compared with the 10 or even 15 years quoted to some customers in 1972. Provided you don't mind the colour there's even a good chance that you could get one ex-stock.

Mulliner, Park Ward is a very important division of Rolls-Royce and wholly owned by them. An amalgamation of two old-established specialist coach-building firms (Park Ward was acquired in 1939, H. J. Mulliner in 1959), this division carries out all the

KMB 716N

body-building and trim work on the Corniche to their own designs. The Corniche is, in effect, a two-door version of the Silver Shadow. Steel pressings for the underbody and floorpan arrive at Mulliner, Park Ward's Willesden factory from Pressed Steel Fisher, where they are modified and strengthened considerably to compensate for the loss of the roof (in the case of the drophead) and the much smaller central side pillar (in the case of the saloon). Mulliner, Park Ward then graft on the body (including a bonnet, boot lid and doors made from aluminium) which is then transported to Rolls-Royce's main factory where it is primed and the mechanical running gear and some of the electrics added. The car is then taken back to Willesden where it is trimmed, painted and finished.

All of which explains in part why the Corniche at £22,826.70 costs £6282.90 more than the equivalent Silver Shadow. The price of exclusiveness derived from a different shape is very high! With more power (though exactly how much Rolls-Royce as usual don't disclose), the Corniche should be considerably faster than its four-door sister; ours wasn't, but we have no reason to doubt Rolls-Royce's assertion that the Corniche should top 120 mph with ease, a claim supported by other independent tests. However, this, and other admittedly small faults, suggests that Rolls-Royce quality control

hasn't yet reached perfection. In other respects, the Corniche is virtually identical to the Shadow, though the facia and instrumentation is slightly more complex and a quadrophonic tape player is fitted as standard. Above all, the two-door arrangement and revised interior design mean that the Corniche is considerably smaller inside than the Shadow, and access to the back seat is quite awkward. The Corniche is more likely, therefore, to appeal to a rich owner-driver than to a person who wishes to be chauffeur-driven. The fact that the Corniche is much more exclusive than the Silver Shadow—less than 500 are built per year out of a total production of nearly 3000 cars—might be a telling factor for some. The even more rare Camargue costs nearly another £9,000.

Although an outrageously expensive car, the prestige and reputation of the marque make any value-for-money assessment rather academic. Make no mistake, the Corniche is a magnificent means of transport even though numerous detail shortcomings, some of them inexcusable in a car costing over £20,000, make that "Best in the World" tag hard to justify. Best at what? Certainly not, for instance, at suppressing road noise over bumps.

Quiet, relaxed cruising is the Corniche's forté; at speed and on smooth roads, it is extremely quiet, though there are competitors available at a fraction of the

cost which nowadays approach the Rolls-Royce's peacefulness. The automatic gearbox is superb, and the ride similarly smooth and refined. Close examination of the car inside and out reveals an attention to detail and workmanship that's sadly often lacking in many massed produced rivals; from the close fit of the body panels to the delicately sculptured switches, it's a real delight to behold. Added to this is an abundance of gadgets that ensure that both driver and passengers are cosseted in the sort of luxury unobtainable elsewhere. Perhaps the Corniche's greatest asset is a very special feeling of one-upmanship; while you're driving your Rolls, albeit an imperfect Rolls, the rest are just in cars.

PERFORMANCE

⭐⭐⭐ The Corniche's engine has remained basically unchanged. In most respects it is identical to the Shadow's—a light alloy 90 deg V8 with pushrod operated overhead valves and hydraulic tappets. It displaces 6475 cc, is slightly oversquare with bore/stroke dimensions of 104.1./99.1 mm and has a compression ratio of 9.0:1. Two SU HD8 carburetters are used, with a mixture weakening device included in the fuel line and an automatic choke for starting. The only significant difference from the Shadow's specification is the adoption of a "hotter" camshaft to produce more power—though exactly how much more, Rolls-Royce as usual aren't revealing.

It must be substantial, though, for it more than offsets the Corniche's extra weight. Our test car lapped MIRA's banked circuit at 116 mph—about 4 mph quicker than the Shadow managed. On a flat road, we would expect the car to do what Rolls-Royce claim —about 120 mph.

Even so, the Corniche is not a super-fast car. Both the Jaguar XJ12 and Mercedes 450 SEL top 130 mph with ease. Academic, perhaps, where there are blanket speed limits, but not in Germany where high speeds are still permitted (and often used).

What the Corniche loses on sheer performance, it offsets with refinement. Some drivers detected a little more rumbling from the engine than they expected at full throttle and high revs, but generally it's very quiet and smooth. When cruising at 100— a mere 3700 rpm for instance— you can't hear the engine above the muted whoosh of wind and tyre noise.

One extremely useful gadget is the automatic speed control (a standard fitting). It consists of a regulator driven from the gearbox, a vacuum-operated bellows that adjusts the throttle and a set of electrical controls on the facia. With the unit switched on, and the car already travelling at a speed convenient for cruising, the driver presses the button marked "engage" to maintain that speed until the unit is disconnected by switching off or applying the brakes. Pressing

"resume" will cause the car gently to accelerate back to the pre-selected speed.

Apart from an initial, neck-jerking surge of acceleration from rest (it's one of the few automatics that we remember spinning its wheels from a standstill on MIRA's very grippy surface), the Corniche's acceleration is not exciting. From rest to 60 mph took 10.7 sec, 100 mph 33.5 sec, sticking to the automatic gearbox's change-up points of 4200 and 4300 rpm. The acceleration tails off noticeably if you hang on any longer. Rolls-Royce weren't too happy with these figures incidentally; they reckon a Corniche should reach 60 mph in under 10 sec and 100 mph in less than 30 sec.

Starting from cold, after the accelerator had been pressed once to the floor to set the automatic choke, was always instantaneous. The warm-up period was quick, and completely free of any troublesome hestitations or hiccoughs. Firing up a hot engine, though, could take a few seconds' cranking, perhaps because of vapour locking in the fuel system under the bonnet.

ECONOMY

⭐ If you can afford to buy a Rolls-Royce at £22,000, it's unlikely you'll be very concerned about the fuel consumption—which is just as well, because our Corniche returned 11.6 mpg overall. With steady speed figures that don't rise above 16 mpg however slowly you go, and a touring figure of 13.8 mpg, you're not going to gain much by gentle driving. We managed 12.5 mpg on a fairly leisurely cross-country journey.

The enormous 24-gallon tank gives no more than a fair range with this sort of thirst. You might get about 330 miles out of one tankful but it's more likely to be substantially less—about 280 miles, which is poor for a trans-continental trip.

TRANSMISSION

⭐⭐⭐⭐ Apart from the first three years of the Shadow's production run, to 1968, all Shadows (and latterly, the Corniche) have used the superb GM 400 automatic gearbox. Unlike the Hydramatic unit fitted originally—which featured four speeds and a fluid coupling—the GM 400 box has the almost universally adopted modern arrangement of three speeds and a torque converter. Considering Rolls-Royce's reputation for sluggish response to technical innovation, it's interesting to note that Mercedes Benz didn't make the same move until three years later.

One unusual feature is the delightful fingertip selector lever. Only Rolls-Royce and some American manufacturers now favour this position, though the gearbox is so good that the necessity for manual selection on the move is minimal; even our most enthusiastic drivers left the lever

Above left: armchair comfort in the front and (above right) in the rear. Access is tricky, though. Left: a daunting sight, but most service items are accessible. Right: the boot held 12.7 cu ft of our suitcases

in Drive for all but the rarest of occasions—descending a steep hill, for instance.

On upward gearchanges, whether when the car is accelerating gently or hard, the gearbox is uncannily smooth. One gear slurs into another with deceptive ease and you often have to check the rev counter to make sure that a change has in fact occurred. With no gaps between the sensibly chosen ratios, and a torque converter whose characteristics ideally suit the engine, the resultant flow of uninterrupted acceleration is both effortless and extremely satisfying.

Should the need arise for some snap acceleration, the gearbox also responds quickly and smoothly to full throttle kickdown. There's nothing so unrefined as a jerk or hesitation here. Only when the selector lever is used to change down manually is the transmission slightly jerky: it's best to cushion the change with a whiff of throttle.

When left to its own devices, the gearbox changes up at 4200 and 4300 rpm on full throttle—corresponding to 45 and 78 mph. We found that these points were just right for best acceleration—there's no point in revving the engine any further. Should the need arise, the engine will spin to 4750 rpm (corresponding to 51 and 86 mph) without fear of anything breaking.

HANDLING

★★☆ In typical Rolls-Royce fashion, the handling of both the Corniche and Shadow models has improved steadily over the years, rather than in a few dramatic leaps forward. At the end of 1972, the front suspension of both models was modified extensively. More

compliance was built into the wishbones to reduce road noise and harder bushes were used in the front sub-frame to improve the handling; at the same time, the steering was made more direct (3¼ turns from lock to lock instead of 3¾) and the rear anti-roll bar increased in thickness. Tyre size has also changed—from the 8.45 x 15 low profile crossplies of 1969, through the 205-15 radials fitted to the Silver Shadow we tested in 1973, to the very much wider 235/70 HR 15 Avon radials that have been standard fittings on all Corniches since October 1974. With the wider tyres came an increase in track of 0.6in at the front and 2.125in at the rear.

The self-levelling system has remained unchanged. It consists of small hydraulic rams mounted above each coil spring (front and rear) that correct any changes in ride height detected by small sensors. When the transmission selection lever is in Neutral or Park, the system responds quickly to a change in trim, but under normal driving conditions the action is much more sluggish so that normal suspension movements aren't affected.

The understeer which characterised previous Rolls-Royce cars, and made them rather tiresome to drive along a twisting road, is much less apparent. Some initial understeer still exists when turning into a corner but it's by no means excessive and helps convey a great feeling of security. As power is applied mid-way through a corner the understeer all but disappears, and on slow corners the tail can even step out of line; if it does, opposite lock is easy to apply. Above all, the roadholding and sheer grip from the tyres allows you to steer round corners at speeds that would have left earlier Rolls-

Royces scrabbling for adhesion.

But our major criticism still remains; the power steering is far too light and lacking in useful feel. Apart from the impossibility of detecting a slippery patch in the wet, it means that most drivers—certainly until they've had a period of acclimatisation—find it difficult to place the car with accuracy. You tend to put too much lock on to start with and then correct in a series of small bites. After a while you learn to turn more progressively into a corner, but that's no real solution. We'd like less assistance and better feel.

BRAKES

★★★ With no less than three separate brake circuits, the Corniche's brake system is about as fail-safe as possible with modern technology. Two circuits are fully powered—that is to say the pedal operates a valve which allows hydraulic fluid to flow to the brakes from the same high pressure reservoir that sustains the ride height adjuster. One of these acts on both the front and rear wheels and contributes 53 per cent of the braking effort while the other operates on the front wheels alone and provides 31 per cent. The third circuit is completely unassisted, affects only the rear brakes and provides the remaining 16 per cent braking effort—and thus ensures that should the high pressure hydraulic system fail completely (an extremely unlikely occurrence) the car can be brought to rest. Discs are fitted front and rear (ventilated at the front) and to accommodate the plethora of hydraulic circuits each front wheel has two two-cylinder calipers and each rear one four-cylinder calipers. Two brake warning lights are provided

to indicate a fault in any of the circuits; the integrity of the electrical connections supplying these can be checked at any time by depressing a special test button.

During our fade test, the pedal pressure required for a 0.5g stop rose from 20 to 28 lb, just enough to be detected subjectively but not enough to worry about. We didn't notice any fade when driving on the road, though, and the disturbing throbbing, almost grating, sound emitted by previous Shadows' brakes when called upon to work hard, was completely absent. In fact, it's when braking hard from high speed that the brakes are most impressive, for the car always pulls up four-square on the road with no hint of juddering or pulling. Some of our drivers thought that they were a little unprogressive at low speed, however, so that to make a smooth stop needs a conscious effort to feather the brake pedal slightly.

The handbrake gave a good 0.37g emergency stop but wouldn't hold the car facing up a 1 in 3 slope. Locking the transmission in Park did the trick, though.

ACCOMMODATION

★★☆ Despite its stately 17ft overall length and 6ft width, the interior accommodation isn't anything special. If the front seats are run (electrically, as always) to their rearmost position, an average-sized adult will find his knees touching the seat backs, while a six-foot adult won't have plenty of room to spare. Despite the large and wide-opening doors, getting in and out of the back isn't the simple step-in affair of the Shadow, either; you have to manoeuvre over a deep sill and through a fairly narrow gap between the back of the front seat (which hinges forward) and the rear quarter panel. For the owner who relies mainly on the services of a chauffeur or carries rear-seat passengers, then, the Shadow is likely to have more appeal; it's significant that most Corniches we've seen on the road have been owner-driven with the rear seats unoccupied.

The seats themselves are comfortable enough, though we'd prefer a lot more lateral and lumbar support for those in the front. The standard leather upholstery doesn't help to hold you in on corners but cloth seats are available for £55.87 extra. As in most Rolls-Royce models, the rear seats are the most comfortable, if only because the central pull-down armrest is larger and softer than that in the front, and headrests are provided as standard.

We managed to squeeze only 12.7 cu ft of our test suitcases into the boot. We say "only" for whereas this would be an enormous figure for most normal cars, it's considerably less than the 14.5 cu ft that the Shadow holds. It's still more than enough for a longish trip to the South of France, though.

There isn't much provision for the stowage of oddments inside the car, however. The glove box (lockable) and shin-bin beneath aren't very big and there isn't a convenient central tray. There's a bin in each door with a map pocket towards the rear but both are a good stretch for a belted-in front-seat passenger.

RIDE

★★★ By normal standards, we'd rate the ride highly. But the Corniche must be judged by absolute standards, which is why we've only given it three stars here—and that's perhaps being generous when the cheapest Jaguar XJ 3.4, costing four times less than the Rolls-Royce, gives a smoother, quieter ride. That of the Corniche is certainly soft and resilient—perhaps too much so, as even on well surfaced roads it tends to float gently up and down, like a ship in a swell. Underlying this movement, which is only evident on long-wavelength undulations, is a muffled but distinct vibration caused by big tyres thumping over sharper humps and depressions like manhole covers, road repair ridges and even Cat Eyes. Slight body shake was also evident over poor surfaces. Uncomfortable? No, far from it. But by Rolls-Royce's standards, disappointing.

AT THE WHEEL

★★ Both front seats are adjustable electrically for height, tilt, and reach, the various motors being controlled by little "joysticks" (one on each door). The backrests have manual adjusters, however. The possible combination of settings is enormous and it takes quite some time to tailor a driving position that's really comfortable. If you're patient it is possible to find a position that's as near to perfection as you'll get. Unfortunately safety regulations have forced the dropping of the Corniche's original 15in wood-rim wheel so that the normal Shadow-style 16in plastic one is used now. A little too large and slippery for our tastes, it is nevertheless well placed, as are the rest of the major controls. The transmission selector lever, for instance, is only a handspan away on the right of the steering column, while the brake pedal can be operated easily with either foot.

Compared to rivals like Mercedes S-class of cars, the facia looks messy and far from ergonomic. The switchgear and instruments are scattered in an apparently haphazard fashion across the shiny (and beautifully made) walnut dashboard. But in fact the arrangement is quite acceptable and certainly a lot better than Rolls-Royce's facias used to be. The stalk on the left of the steering column controls the indicators and headlamp flasher while pressing its end operates the washers and wipers simultaneously. The master light

MOTOR ROAD TEST No 56/75 ● Rolls-Royce Corniche

PERFORMANCE

CONDITIONS
Weather	Wind 0-10 mph
Temperature	60-65°F
Barometer	29.5 in. Hg
Surface	Dry tarmac

MAXIMUM SPEEDS
	mph	kph
Banked circuit	116.0	186.6
Best ¼ mile	118.4	190.5
Terminal speeds:		
at ¼ mile	78	126
at kilometre	99	159
Speed in gears (at 4750 rpm):		
1st	51	82
2nd	86	138

ACCELERATION FROM REST
mph	sec		sec
0-30	3.4	0-40	2.6
0-40	5.3	0-60	4.8
0-50	7.7	0-80	7.7
0-60	10.7	0-100	11.5
0-70	14.2	0-120	16.0
0-80	18.6	0-140	22.8
0-90	25.1	0-160	33.3
0-100	33.5		
Stand'g ¼	17.8	Stand'g km	32.6

ACCELERATION IN KICKDOWN
mph	sec	kph	sec
20-40	3.4	40-60	2.2
30-50	4.3	60-80	2.9
40-60	5.4	80-100	3.8
50-70	6.5	100-120	4.5
60-80	7.9	120-140	6.8
70-90	10.9	140-160	10.5
80-100	14.9		

FUEL CONSUMPTION
Touring*	13.8 mpg
	20.5 litres/100 km
Overall	11.6 mpg
	24.4 litres/100 km
Fuel grade	100 octane
	5 star rating
Tank capacity	24.0 galls
	109.0 litres
Max range	331 miles
	533 km
Test distance	1676 miles
	2697 km

*Consumption midway between 30 mph and maximum less 5 per cent for acceleration.

BRAKES
Pedal pressure deceleration and stopping distance from 30 mph (48 kph)
lb	kg	g	ft	m
25	11	0.57	53	16
50	23	1.00+	30	9
Handbrake	0.37		81	25

FADE
20 ½g stops at 1 min intervals from speed midway between 40 mph (64 kph) and maximum (76 mph, 122 kph)
	lb	kg
Pedal force at start	20	9
Pedal force at 10th stop	24	11
Pedal force at 20th stop	28	13

STEERING
Turning circle between kerbs
	ft	m
left	35.3	10.8
right	34.4	10.5
Lock to lock	3.35 turns	
50ft diam circle	1.15 turns	

SPEEDOMETER (mph)
Speedo	30	40	50	60	70	80	90	100
True mph	31	41	51	61	70½	80½	90½	100½

Distance recorder: accurate

WEIGHT
	cwt	kg
Unladen weight*	43.5	2210
Weight as tested	47.2	2398

*with fuel for approx 50 miles

Performance tests carried out by Motor's staff at the Motor Industry Research Association proving ground, Lindley.

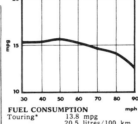

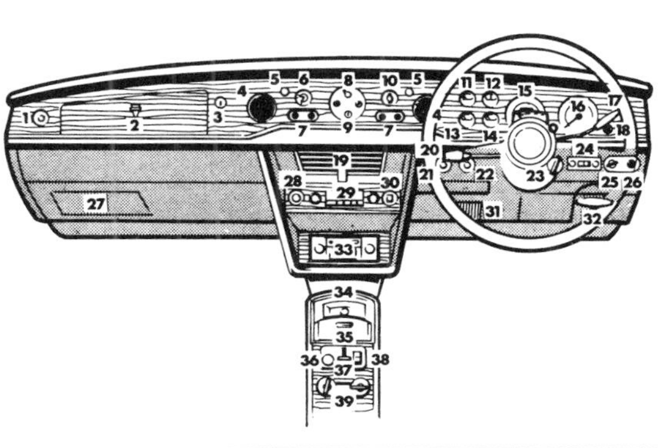

1 map reading light switch
2 glove box
3 glove box lock
4 air conditioning vents
5 volume controls for 4
6 clock
7 warning lights
8 light switch
9 ignition lock
10 wash/wipe switch
11 fuel gauge
12 ammeter
13 coolant temperature gauge
14 oil pressure gauge
15 speedometer
16 rev counter
17 transmission selector
18 handbrake warning light
19 air conditioning vent
20 wash/wipe/indicator/headlamp

21 flasher stalk
22 "test" button
22 filler cap release button
23 parking light switch
24 speed control
25 panel light rheostat
26 roof light switch
27 shin bin
28 radio balance control
29 radio
30 radio aerial switch
31 bonnet release
32 handbrake
33 quadrophonic tape player
34 cigar lighter
35 ashtray
36 hazard warning light switch
37 fan switch
38 heated backlight switch
39 air conditioning controls

COMPARISONS

	Capacity cc	Price £	Max mph	0-60 sec	30-50* sec	Overall mpg	Touring mpg	Length ft in	Width ft in	Weight cwt	Boot cu ft
Rolls-Royce Corniche	6750	22,827	116.8	11.1	4.2	11.6	13.9	16 11.5	5 11.8	43.5	12.7
Fiat 130 Coupe	3235	7455	115.6	10.6	3.9	18.8	—†	15 10	6 0	31.7	12.3
Jensen Interceptor	7212	9629	129.0	7.7	2.7	10.0	15.6	15 8	5 10	34.8	8.5
Mercedes-Benz 450 SEL	4520	10,773	131.0	9.3	4.0	14.0	—†	16 9.5	6 1.5	34.6	15.0
Panther De Ville	5343	22,950	—‡	9.5	3.5	12.1	—‡	16 11.9	5 11.1	38.3	—‡
Rolls-Royce Silver Shadow	6750	16,544	112.4	10.3	4.0	10.9	15.9	17 0	5 11	41.4	14.5
Vanden Plas Daimler Double Six	5343	8437	135.7	7.4	2.6	11.5	13.5	15 10	4 11	34.8	11.8

*in kickdown †not measured—cars fitted with fuel injection ‡not measured—car subject of feature test only

Test Data · World copyright reserved; no unauthorised reproduction in whole or in part.

MOTOR ROAD TEST No 56/75 ● Rolls-Royce Corniche

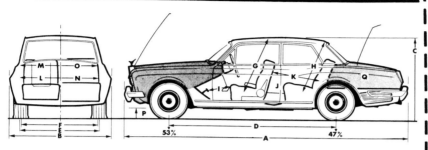

		ft	in	cm			ft	in	cm
A	overall 'length	16	11½	517	K	front to back			
B	overall width	6	0	183		seat max	2	10	86
C	unladen height	4	10½	149		min	2	6	76
D	wheelbase	9	11½	304	L	front elbow			
E	front track	4	11½	151		width	4	6	137
F	rear track	4	9½	147	M	front shoulder			
G	com. seat to					width	4	6	137
	roof front	3	0	91	N	rear elbow			
H	com. seat to					width	3	11½	308
	roof rear	2	10	86	O	rear shoulder			
I	pedal to seat					width	4	5	135
	max	1	4	41	P	min ground			
	min	1	0	30		clearance		6½	17
J	kneeroom max	1	2	36	Q	boot capacity	12.7 cu ft		
	min		10	25					

GENERAL SPECIFICATION

ENGINE
Cylinders — V8
Capacity — 6750 cc (411.9 cu in.)
Bore/stroke — 104.1/99.0 mm (4.10/3.90 in.)
Cooling — Water
Block — Aluminium alloy
Head — Aluminium alloy
Valves — Pushrod ohv, hydraulic tappets
Valve timing
Inlet opens — 10¼° btdc
Inlet closes — 75½° abcd
ex opens — 52½° bbdc
ex closes — 33½° atdc
Compression — 9.0 : 1
Carburetter — Twin SU HD8
Bearings — 5 main
Fuel pump — Twin SU electric
Max power — Not disclosed
Max torque — Not disclosed
TRANSMISSION
Type — 3-speed automatic gearbox (GM Type 400) plus torque converter.

Internal ratios and mph/1000 rpm
Top — 1.00 : 1/26.9
2nd — 1.48 : 1/18.2

1st — 2.48 : 1/10.8
Rev — 2.08 : 1
Final drive — 3.08 : 1
BODY/CHASSIS
Construction — Unitary
Protection — Zinc-coated steel in vulnerable areas plus underseal
SUSPENSION
Front — Independent by double wishbones, coils, telescopic dampers and anti-roll bar. Automatic height control
Rear — Independent by semi-trailing arms, coils, telescopic dampers and anti-roll bar. Automatic height control
STEERING
Type — Recirculating ball
Assistance — Yes
Toe in — 0.060 - 0.160 in. at 17 in. dia
Camber — −0° 30′ ± 0° 15′
Castor — +3° 0′ ± 0° 15′

King pin — 11° 0′
Rear toe-in — 0.00 - 0.060 in. at 17 in. dia
Rear camber — −0° 30′ ± 0° 15′
BRAKES
Type — Rolls-Royce discs front and rear
Servo — Two high pressure pumps supplying hydraulic reservoir
Circuit — Triple: two high pressure; one direct-acting
Rear valve — Deceleration-sensitive valve
Adjustment — Automatic
WHEELS
Type — Pressed steel 15 in. x 6 in.
Tyres — Avon radial 235/70 HR 15
Pressures — 25 psi
ELECTRICAL
Battery — 12 v, 71 Ah
Polarity — Negative
Generator — Alternator
Fuses — 20
Headlights — 75w (Inner) 37½/60w (Outer)

STANDARD EQUIPMENT

Adjustable steering	No	Head restraints	**Rear only**
Anti-lock brakes	No	Heated rear window	Yes
Armrests	Seven	Laminated screen	Yes
Ashtrays	Five	Lights	
Breakaway mirror	Yes	Boot	Yes
Cigar lighter	Three	Courtesy	Yes
Childproof locks	No	Engine bay	Yes
Clock	Yes	Hazard warning	Yes
Coat hooks	No	Map reading	Yes
Dual circuit brakes	Triple	Parking	Yes
Electric windows	Yes	Reversing	Yes
Energy absorb steering col	Yes	Spot/fog	Yes
Fresh air ventilation	Yes	Locker	Yes
Grab handles	Three	Outside mirror	Yes

Parcel shelf	No
Petrol filler lock	Yes
Radio	Yes
Rev counter	Yes
Seat belts	
Front	Yes
Rear	No
Seat recline	Yes
Seat height adjuster	Yes
Sliding roof	No
Tinted glass	**Yes—if requested**
Combination wash/wipe	Yes
Wipe delay	Yes
Vanity mirror	Yes

IN SERVICE

GUARANTEE
Duration ... **Three years or 50,000 miles on mechanical parts; one year on coachwork**

MAINTENANCE
Schedule .... every 6000 miles
First service .... at 3000 miles

DO-IT-YOURSELF
Sump .... 14.5 pints, SAE 20W/50
Gearbox .... 18.6 pints, Dexron
Rear axle ...... 4.5 pints, SAE 90 EP
Steering gear .... 3 pints, Dexron
Coolant .... 28.5 pints
Chassis lubrication ... 5 points every 12,000 miles
Distributor dwell angle 26-28 deg
Spark plug type ... Champion N14Y
Spark plug gap .... 0.025 in.
Tappets .... **Not adjustable**

REPLACEMENT COSTS
Brake pads/linings (front) £7.37
Complete exhaust system £257.42
Engine (exchange) £1126.72
Damper (front) £12.20
Front wing £200.00
Gearbox (new) £317.08
Oil filter £3.00
Starter motor £76.00
Windscreen £86.20

Make: Rolls-Royce
Model: Corniche
Maker: Rolls-Royce Motors Ltd, Crewe, Cheshire, CW1 3PL
Price: £19,510.00 plus £1,625.83 car tax and £1,690.87 VAT equals £22,826.70.

switch is mounted right in the centre of the facia above the ignition key with the normal wash/wipe switch a few inches to its right; the dipswitch is sited on the floor to the left of the brake pedal. The rest of the switches are arranged along the bottom roll of the facia on the right of the steering wheel: parking lights, speed control, panel light rheostat and interior roof light. All the switches look attractive and have a neat, precise action that make them particularly satisfying to use.

Like the Shadow, the Corniche has its ungainly pull-out handbrake mounted below the facia on the right—just where it can give your knee a nasty crack when getting in and out of the car, particularly if you're tall.

The Corniche has very thin pillars behind the doors, too thin for mounting sufficiently strong seat belt anchorages. Rolls-Royce have therefore mounted the top mount on the waistline, a position which makes the belt is intolerably difficult to find and put on, and infuriatingly prone to slipping off when in use. A roof mount used in conjunction with a slave arm which ensures that the diagonal doesn't cut across your neck (as on the new Opel Manta tested last week) would be far better.

VISIBILITY

★★★ Because of the excellent amount of seat adjustment provided, you can sit high up and with a commanding view over the bonnet and front wings. Consequently, the Corniche is a lot easier to drive through crowded city streets than its bulk—and measurements—might suggest. A door mirror on the driver's side—adjustable from within—is provided as standard but the view rearwards is generally poor, mostly because of the bulky and obstructive headrests in the rear. Reversing in a tight situation can thus be a headache.

The wipers clear only a small area of the screen and tend to lift off at high speed. Like the Jaguar XJ3.4 we tested a few weeks ago, the wipers have a special mechanism intended to make them park out of the normal arc of use. We found the hesitation that this entailed irritating, while the wipers invariably didn't park flush with the bottom of the screen anyway. The headlamps give a beam that's adequate for the car's performance.

INSTRUMENTS

★★★★ With a speedometer (incorporating a trip recorder as well as the normal odometer), a rev counter, an ammeter and water temperature, oil pressure and fuel gauges, as well as a clock, the Corniche has a full complement of instruments.

The speedometer is mounted directly in front of the driver, the rev counter to its right with the

Above: typical Rolls-Royce decor with walnut facia, lambswool carpets and leather upholstery. Below left: personal controls for each rear seat passenger include lighter and ashtray, window and light switches. Below right : superbly made door trims. Note the adjustable armrest

four minor instruments on the left. They're all beautifully calibrated (and judging by the two whose performance we were able to check—the speedometer and rev counter—remarkably accurate, too) but stray reflections from their glass faces and the surrounding polished wood facia make them difficult to read in daylight. At night, there's no trouble with reflections and all the instruments are illuminated with an admirably restful and diffused light.

Warning lights are also provided for low fuel level, high coolant temperature, brake failure, low charge, and low oil pressure. A button allows these warning lights to be tested and when depressed indicates the sump oil level on the fuel gauge.

HEATING

★★
★★ Air conditioning is, of course, supplied as standard. It's certainly one of the best around (barring that fitted to the Camargue) and incorporates no fewer than 11 separate electric motors to move the hidden flaps and valves. Apart from the four-speed fan, two controls are supplied which determine the quantity and temperature of the air to the upper and lower halves of the car. The basic rule of these controls is pull for quantity and turn for temperature, but they can be a little confusing at first.

The "lower" air is channelled to the footwells alone and can only be heated or supplied at ambient temperature. The "upper" air goes to the windscreen, and also to two eyeball vents and a large "chip-cutter" grille in the centre of the facia; it can be heated or refrigerated. The eyeballs can be adjusted finely for volume and direction, while the grille has a volume control that's essentially an on/off switch; it's particularly useful for channelling refrigerated air to the rear passengers in hot weather.

The Corniche's stay with Motor coincided with the August heatwave so that we had very little chance to assess the heating. We know from our tests of Shadows that the system is most effective once learnt and a powerful blast

of hot air is available whenever you need it. It's also easy to obtain warm air to your feet and cold—even near-freezing—air to your face should you so desire. But it is possible to set the controls wrong and, as with so many other air conditioning systems, mist up the windows in a flash, particularly in foggy weather; it only happened to us once, though.

VENTILATION

★★
★★ With refrigerated air available to your face and upper body at any time, the air conditioning is most effective in hot weather. But it's also controllable enough so that if a trickle of tepid air is required it's easily arranged.

If the air conditioning is turned to a lower temperature setting and also when starting the engine after the car has been at a standstill, the facia outlets can emit an unpleasant, initial blast of air until the system purges. Switching the fan on full minimises this.

NOISE

★★
★★ Although exceptionally quiet by normal standards, the Rolls-Royce Corniche is very far from silent. By far the most prominent noise is the bumping and thumping of the tyres over coarse or broken surfaces. Even that's reasonably well muffled when judged by any standards other than those set by Peugeot and Jaguar. You can hear the engine when under hard acceleration and at high rpm, and

you can hear some hissing from the door seals at high speeds— but you only really notice this because the car is so quiet at other times. Noise from other sources is very low. The whirring of the various heater/air conditioning motors is much less audible than in early Rolls-Royce installations of similar design, and the electric window motors are almost silent, as well as very quick in action.

FINISH

★★
★★ For £20,000 you expect something special in terms of craftsmanship and we doubt that anyone would be disappointed with the finish of a Corniche. All the body panels, engine castings and trim fitments had obviously been designed and fashioned with extreme care. Our car, however, did have a number of detail faults. The doors were difficult to open and close, and tended to rattle if slammed. Other niggling imperfections were a torn door seal on the driver's side, some oozing gum around the top edge of that seal, and a cigar lighter and main-beam tell tale that didn't work.

The interior appearance is traditional Rolls-Royce: polished walnut for the facia, centre consoles and door cappings, Connolly hide leather for the seats and door trims and lamb's wool rugs on the floor over the beautifully fitting short pile carpet. Should you so desire you can specify a leather headlining (£115.83) or cloth upholstery instead.

EQUIPMENT

★★
★★ It's almost superfluous to say that the list of standard equipment is very long indeed. As well as fairly normal items such as air conditioning, electric windows, a clock, a heated rear window, an outside mirror and lights for the boot, engine bay and parking, there is a veritable array of gadgets (not gimmicks) to ensure that both the driver and passengers are cosseted in ultimate luxury. The interior light remains on for a few seconds after closing the door, for instance, giving the driver time to insert his key in the ignition switch. The fuel filler door is released by pressing a button on the facia, so that you need never stir from your seat at the filling station. The boot and both doors can be locked by central switches on each door. But the boot can only be unlocked electrically by a switch inside the lockable cubby in front of the passenger. This means that you can leave valuables safely in the boot and glove locker while the car is being serviced, if you remove the common glove locker and boot key. Incorporated in the lid of the locker is a stand-up mirror.

The electric windows incorporate an interesting, but fiddly, safety characteristic. To minimise the chances of fingers being trapped, the normal window switch only makes the window close to within one inch of its seal. A separate switch is then used for the final travel.

Not the least of the Corniche's fixtures are the stereo FM/AM radio, complete with electric aerial, and full quadraphonic cartridge player, both again supplied as standard.

Another interesting feature of the Corniche is the profusion of appointments for smokers. In the front there's a voluminous ashtray behind the central cigar lighter as well as a separate ashtray on each door, while in the rear each passenger has an ashtray and a cigar lighter.

IN SERVICE

An initial service is required at 3000 miles, after which servicing is needed only every 12,000 miles apart from an oil change and safety check at 6000 miles. Most filling station points such as the dipstick (for engine and automatic transmission), water cap and washer bottle are easily accessible. The battery is in the boot.

Though we doubt whether any owners would carry out their own servicing, the engine compartment isn't as cluttered as a cursory glance may suggest. A plug change may require a tool with a universal joint but apart from that there appear to be few problems.

Rolls-Royce provide a particularly well thought-out and high quality tool kit that's normally stowed above the battery. It even includes such items as a tyre pressure gauge, feeler gauges and spare bulbs.

OWNER'S VIEW

OWNERS VIEW

Racing driver Gerry Marshall has owned many examples of the Rolls-Royce Corniche and its close relative, the Silver Shadow, not only in the course of his everyday business buying and selling quality cars, but as personal vehicles.

C.H. How do you rate a new Corniche for the first-time buyer?
G.M. They offer excellent value for money provided you have that much money! It's always worth considering buying the most exclusive variant on an established theme, although in this case, I think that a Corniche might be a more attractive proposition than, say, a Camargue – which is basically the same car – because, after all, with the Corniche you can still lower the hood. I would say also that it has to be admitted that there has been a considerable sales resistance to the appearance of the Camargue. The Corniche looks far less controversial and more like what you would expect of a Rolls-Royce.

C.H. How do you rate a Corniche as a second-hand buy?
G.M. They can be far more attractive than new, simply because they are now far cheaper! The main stipulation here, of course, is that the car must have been maintained immaculately, which means bodywork as well as mechanical attention. You have to be prepared for some big bills if the car has been neglected or mistreated. It is possible, however, to make quite accurate estimates as to how much a Corniche would cost to restore to pristine condition, and then have the work done, because the resale price is sufficiently high to allow a realistic amount of money to be spent. It's not like looking at a cheap family car, the value of which can never justify how much might have to be spent on it.
C.H. What would you say were the really good points about a Corniche as opposed to a Silver Shadow?
G.M. Apart from the obvious desirability of having such an exclusive car, rather than a Silver Shadow which might be just like that of one or many business associates, it is the fact that even with the earliest Corniches, all the points that might have been questionable about the Silver Shadow seem to have been ironed out. The suspension changes, for instance, in conjunction with radial-ply tyres, made the most difference. Directional stability was much improved and the Corniche became a lot more manageable at speed. It

did not wander off course like the early Silver Shadows and the steering became a great deal more responsive. That was improved even further when the rack and pinion was fitted on the series II. It is also well worth trying higher tyre pressures on the Corniche if you feel the cornering and stability can be improved at the expense of the ultimate smoothness of the ride. As much as 25 per cent can be added to the normal pressure without the ride becoming too harsh. The Hydramatic gearbox is so good too, that it puts the old four-speed in the early Shadow in the shade! I must say, also, that I like the idea of having air conditioning as standard, even with the drop-head coupé. There are always a lot of days in Britain – and other countries – when it is hot and sticky, but even worse with the hood down in a heavy traffic jam. At times like that, the insulation that the drop-head Corniche's hood gives you, without having the swelter at the same time, really has to be appreciated!
C.H. What are your favourite aspects of owning a Corniche?
G.M. Well, apart from the good points I've mentioned, there is the solid dependability of the cars, and the sheer value for money that they can offer in second-hand form, or even new if your business is strong enough. Without a doubt, there is also the prestige that such a vehicle offers the majority of owners. In the circles in which they move, the Corniche also represents solid good taste, which can make it even more attractive.
C.H. And what do you consider might be the bad points?
G.M. With the obvious proviso that they have been cared for in the right way – it is a crying shame if they have not – the main problem for most people is actually finding one for sale! Dealers like myself snap them up if they represent the value that will not cause problems or lose future custom, so it's no good scouring the advertisement columns of the local newspaper for a Corniche!

BUYING

The main problem when buying a Rolls-Royce Corniche is actually finding one for sale to the desired specification. They are much rarer than the Silver Shadows on which they are based, of course, with only about 7,000 having been built, the vast majority of which carried the Rolls-Royce radiator grille and badging rather than that of the Bentley subsidiary. Silver Shadows, which were phased out in 1980 to be replaced by the Silver Spirit, are, by comparison, far more plentiful, with about 28,000 having been made, around 3,000 of which were long-wheelbase variants and Mulliner, Park Ward, or James Young, special-bodied cars. The relative exclusivity enhances values of course, apart from the superior specification of the Corniche, with the result that such cars tend to fetch around one-third more than the equivalent Silver Shadow. The fixed-head variants of the Corniche are usually worth at least as much as the drop-heads because very few were made before they were discontinued in 1980, and their interior tends to be better preserved because it has not been exposed to so much sun and wind.

One of the main stipulations to make when buying a Corniche is to insist on seeing a detailed service history. The cars are not only expensive to buy, but very expensive to maintain properly. Should they be serviced in the proper manner, however, they will last almost indefinitely as there is a strong element of preventative work in the recommended Rolls-Royce procedures. The most expensive services occur every 48,000 miles when the car's hydraulic system should come under the most penetrating scrutiny. This generally means replacing belts, hoses and so on, which can cost a lot in parts alone. This is because Rolls-Royce spares are of comparable cost to the price of a new car. On the other hand, they are of extremely good quality and they are in excellent supply – in stark contrast to the position with many lesser cars. But it should be borne in mind that even as this book was being written in 1983, a new chromium-plated bumper bar costs in the order of £700 and a full service in the region of £2,000. In addition, tyre life is short on the early models, with replacement often being necessary at 10,000-mile intervals; later models, particularly the series II, are far better in this respect, the tyre life having been extended to double the earlier figure. The main reason for this is that the cars are heavy and so much attention has been paid to the quality of the ride that the tyres have to work hard. So do the brakes, with an average pad life of between 10,000 and 15,000 miles. Most of this wear is concentrated on the front, the rear pads lasting longer. The discs also need to be replaced quite often, sometimes because of corrosion around the edges caused by salt solution on wintry roads, and on other occasions because of warping as the result of the tremendous heat generated in stopping such a heavy car.

The engine – which does not encourage do-it-yourself maintenance with its sparking plugs well buried in common with those of most V8s – should run for more than 100,000 miles without undue attention. In common with most alloy units, the valve gear can be noisy when it is cold, but it should be extremely quiet in operation once the engine has been warmed fully. If the valve gear is still noisy then, the engine probably needs rebuilding, which can be an expensive business if many parts are required. An exchange unit costs about the same price as the average small car when it is new. Beware also of an oily exhaust as this can be a good indication of engine wear and substantial bills to come. It is vital, also, to be confident that the right type of coolant inhibitor has been used, otherwise the passages in the cylinder heads and block can become corroded. The three-speed General Motors transmission has a wonderful reputation for durability, and should last longer than the engine. In the event of its needing major repairs or replacement, the cost is not great – about half that of a major service.

Like most hydraulic systems, that of the Corniche is expensive to repair, so that any leaks must be viewed with the greatest of suspicion; they warrant immediate attention. A Corniche should also gain its normal ride height as soon as it is started.

Wear in the bushes of the front and rear suspension and in the Metalastik mountings and anti-roll bar supports can have an adverse effect on the handling of a Corniche; such parts are worth regular replacement. Although expensive, the shock absorbers should last between 40,000 and 50,000 miles. For these reasons alone, it is wise to know the full service history of any secondhand Corniche; one having been maintained by relatively unskilled hands, or not maintained at all, being a potentially expensive restoration job.

Body maintenance is as important as that needed by the mechanical components if a Corniche is to retain its value and continue to give the pleasure its owner deserves. It is a fallacy to assume that just because it is a Rolls-Royce, it will last forever, although such is the quality of the paintwork and anti-corrosion measures that the body suffers less than that of many cars. Nevertheless, the common areas for corrosion, around the lower perimeter of the car, are the first to suffer, particularly the sills and the areas behind the wheels. The lead loading beneath the panel joints collapses gradually in old age, leading to cracks in the paint and subsequent corrosion if it is not repaired. Corrosion can also occur as the result of the reaction of the different metals used for brightwork and the alloy of the doors and bonnet. But the most common cause of panel problems with the Corniche is where accident damage has not been properly repaired. The quality of the coachline can be a good indication of unskilled attention in some areas, as can be the gaps between the bonnet, doors, boot lid and surrounding panels. New wings and similar items for a Rolls-Royce are very expensive, with the result that some dubious repairs can be attempted to damaged items. The original paintwork is also of such good quality that it is hard to match and frequently a car should have been completely resprayed rather than just subject to localised repainting. Such repairs are often good enough for ordinary cars, but soon show up by comparison with the original finish.

The woodwork is of superb quality, but can suffer from the effects of the sun like any other, particularly in areas such as Southern California, where the temperatures can be very high after only a short time parked with the hood down. The facia roll and door topping are usually the first places to suffer in these circumstances. The leather upholstery is of marvellous quality as well, but it needs to be maintained properly. Its makers, Connolly, can restore it, but it is an expensive business if there is much deterioration. The hoods on drop-head cars are also expensive to replace, but it is not a difficult job for experienced workers.

Finally, do not necessarily be put off by the number of owners a Corniche might have had. First-time buyers often tend to be large companies which change their cars for prestige reasons on average every two years; there was a time, also, only a few years ago, that the waiting list for a new Rolls-Royce, particularly a Corniche, was so long that secondhand examples commanded a substantial premium. Many owners put in their orders long in advance and simply replaced their Corniche when a new one was ready ... having run the original one for what amounted to nothing in the meantime! Second buyers were often smaller companies and it is usually a question of a car being third or fourth-hand before the private buyer enters on the scene. With their superior tax position, companies more often than not maintained their vehicles properly ...

CLUBS, SPECIALISTS & BOOKS

Clubs

There is one chief club for the owners of Rolls-Royce (and Bentley) Corniches, the **Rolls-Royce Enthusiasts' Club,** the general secretary of which is Lieut Col. E.B. Barrass, of 6 Montacute Road, Tunbridge Wells, Kent, TN2 5QP, England (telephone Tunbridge Wells 26072). The Club's permanent headquarters are at Paulerspury in Northamptonshire in the Sir Henry Royce Memorial Foundation building, which houses a museum, lecture room, library and archives, and a workshop.

Although the Enthusiasts' Club has a worldwide membership both the U.S.A and Australia have their own independent clubs as follows:

The Rolls-Royce Owners' Club Inc. U.S.A. P.O. Box 2001, Mechanicsburg, Pennsylvania, ZIP 17055, U.S.A.

The Rolls-Royce Owners' Club of Australia 34 Jouberts Street, Hunters Hill, 2110, NSW, Australia

Specialists

There are numerous specialists dealing with the marque, including Rolls-Royce appointed agents throughout the world. In Britain alone, there are, in addition, the following well-established specialists: A and S Engineering, Farnham, Surrey; Adams and Oliver, Huntingdon; Aline Eagle, Clanfield, Oxon; A Archer, Great Dunmow, Essex; Ashton Keynes Vintage Restorations, Wilts; Auto Components, Hinckley, Leics; Balmoral Automobile, London SE27; William R Bastow, London NW5; S Brunt, Newcastle, Staffs; Coldwell Engineering, Sheffield; The Cooke Group, Wigston, Leics; Crailville Motors, Southall, Middx; Doug Elliott Restorations, Dagenham, Essex; Michael Freeman, Stroud, Glos; Duncan Hamilton, Bagshot, Surrey; Haines and Hall, London SW8; Healey Bros, Wellingborough, Northants; Robert Holyoak Engineering, Great Glen, Leics; Home Counties Car Spares, Rickmansworth, Herts; Ideal Motors, Brizworth, Northants; JMF Motors, London NW3; Peter Last, London SW6; Laurence Kayne (Ascot), London W1; Lenham Motor Co, Maidstone, Kent; Lipscombe and Hessey, Windsor, Berks; Gerry Marshall, Hemel Hempstead, Herts; McKenzie Guppy, Wimborne, Dorset; Paddon Bros, London SW7; Phillips Garage, Birmingham; Gerry Porter, London SW7; Servicecentre Systems, St Ives, Cambs; Steel Transpositions, London SW7; Michael Walker, Surrey.

Books

Surprisingly, there have been no previous books covering the Corniche specifically, although there have been two which include information on the closely-related Silver Shadows, which also touch on the Corniche. They are:

Rolls-Royce Silver Shadow, Corniche, Camargue, Silver Wraith II and Bentley T by John Bolster. Published by Osprey. An affectionately-written brief history of the cars named in its title.

Rolls-Royce 75 Years: 1904-1979 Published by Rolls-Royce Motors. A condensed picture booklet.

PHOTO
GALLERY

1. In the early 1970s the Corniche's popularity was such that the waiting time for a new car stretched to years, and the auction price of used examples often commanded double the list price.

2

3

2. The classic configuration for the Corniche with hood and windows down. This is a 1972 series I model.

3. Although ostensibly an owner/driver car, the deep hood sides allow travel in privacy for rear seat passengers, should the need arise.

4. For those warmer, or less blustery days, the windows can be retracted complete with chrome surrounds, at the touch of a button.

5

5. Especially for the front seat occupants, driving with the hood down but windows erect allows open-air motoring even in the colder seasons.

6

7

6.   The front of the machine is as impressive and
unmistakable as ...

7.   ... the rear is elegant and simple.

8

8. The series II model was introduced in 1977. Immediately evident is the discontinuation of the brake-cooling air intakes below the headlamps and the deep bumper fitted with a wrap-around rubber over-rider.

9. The furled hood is neatly concealed by a tailored cover.

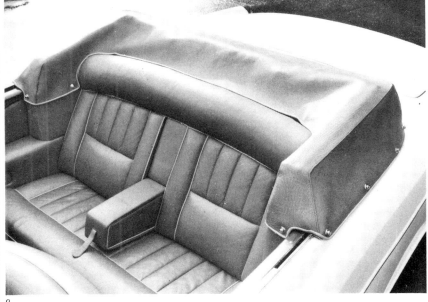

9

10. On removing the cover the ...

11. ... hood can be raised electrically and ...

12. ... latched securely to the windscreen top member.

11

12

13

13. The obvious and essential difference between the Rolls-Royce and ...

14. ... Bentley versions of the Corniche. The Bentley is a very rare beast, only about 100 each of convertible and saloon being built.

14

15 & 16.   On introduction of the series II model for
1977 positioning of the driving lamps was changed and
a spoiler fitted below the bumper.

17 & 18.   The bumper too was modified, to comply with the U.S. regulations. The bumper gap closing panels can be seen to be mounted above the bumper to allow movement of the bumper, provision for which is made in the mounting on U.S. cars.

17

18

19

19.   The air intakes were discontinued in 1973 when it was found that the additional cooling air supply to the brakes was not, in fact, required.

20 & 21.   Wheel arch flares became more pronounced in 1974 with the adoption of a new low-profile tyre.

22.   The driver's door mirror is fitted as standard to all series.

20

21

22

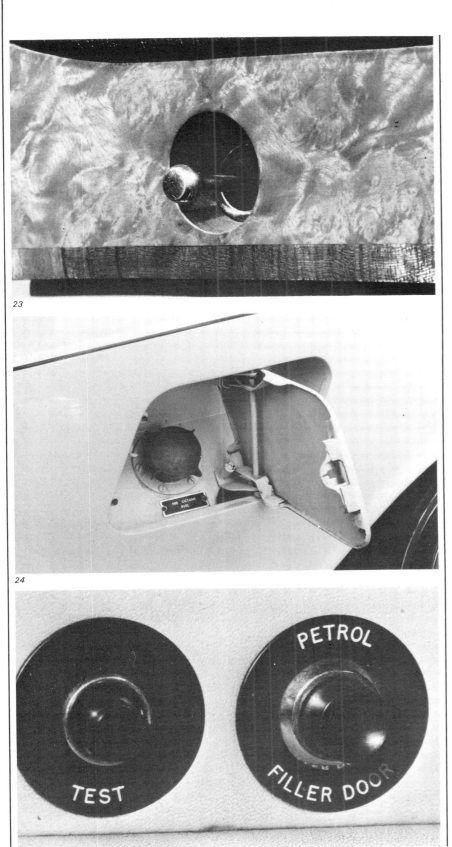

23

24

25

23. *Adjustment to the mirror is made via a remote knob.*

24. *Access to the fuel filler can be made by opening the security panel which is ...*

25. *... released by this dash-mounted button.*

26

27

26 & 27.   Differentiation of marque, when seen from
the rear, could hardly be more discreet.

28.   Separate inset reversing lamps are standard on all
models

28

29. The boot is cavernous, but uncluttered with the ...

30. ... battery concealed on the left.

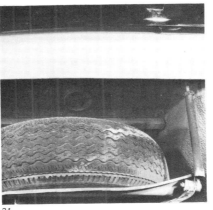

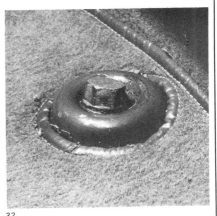

29

30

31

32

31. The spare wheel is concealed beneath the boot floor and is ...

32. ... released by this jacking screw

33. The interior of the series I model. Included in the instrumentation is a tachometer (extra right).

33

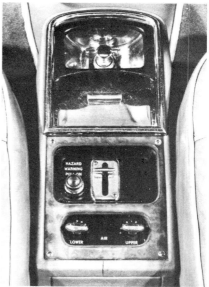

34

35

36

34.   The radio and the cassette player are fitted in the centre console with ...

35.   ... air conditioning controls, hazard warning light switch and ashtray between the seats.

36.   The sporting wood-rimmed steering wheel on the Corniche series I was replaced by ...

37.   ... a smaller two-spoked version on Series II models. The gear selector remained the same, however, although the series II gearbox was a new item.

37

38

38. A newly designed instrument panel was introduced with the series II, the tachometer being discontinued because it was felt to be unnecessary with the new gearbox. The main new instrument was the combined ammeter, oil gauge, water temperature indicator and fuel gauge.

39. A clock and temperature gauge occupied the centre of the new dash panel, with a modified console for air conditioning outlets and in-car entertainment.

40. The ignition lock and lighting switch panel was moved to the outside of the instrument panel with a warning light panel, including ice-alert sensor, next to it.

41 & 42. The small glove compartment on the series I was superseded by a larger item on the series II.

39

40

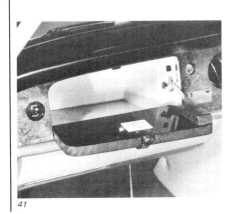

41

42

43

43.	Extensive padding, extending to the sun visor, was used around the windscreen frame on the series II.

44.	Items such as a small lidded tray beside the driver's right hand positively beg the ash from a cigar. A grand total of five ashtrays and three cigar lighters is provided for the occupants' comfort.

45.	Stereo speakers are fitted to the wall of the tidy-locker sunk into each door. A small courtesy lamp is fitted to the roof of the locker.

46.	The traditional, pleated, pocket provides for such things as maps.

44

45

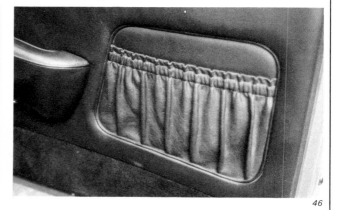

46

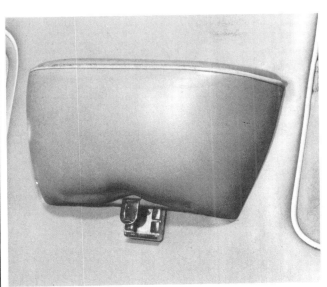

47

48

47. The door pull combined with a convenient adjustable armrest.

48. A tiny red light is incorporated in the trailing edge of each door to warn the unwary that their path might be obstructed.

49

50

49. Each front seat is adjustable electrically for height, tilt and reach, the ...

50. ... control being achieved using this small, door-mounted 'joystick' and fore-aft control switch.

51.

51. Depress the chromed button and ...

52. ... tilt the seat forward to gain access to the rear passenger seat on the same side.

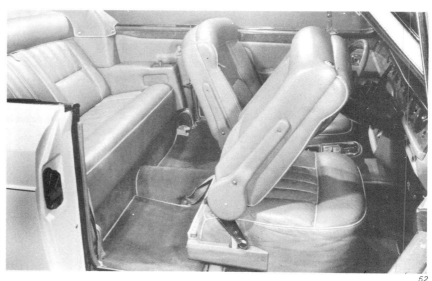

52

53. The series II Corniche was fitted with adjustable head rests.

54. The rear seats provide the level of comfort expected of a Rolls-Royce.

53

54

55

56

55. Each rear seat passenger is provided with his own ashtray, cigar lighter and window control switch. On saloon models these are supplemented by individual lights and light switches.

56. The Mulliner Park Ward nameplate which adornes the sill tread-plate is often accompanied by a similar plate bearing the name of the original supplier.

57 & 58. The 6.7 litre V8 engine which produces what has so often been described as 'ample' power.

57

58

59

60

59. The series II engine is dominated by the massive air cleaner assembly. Also evident are the tops of the revised front suspension assemblies, each side of the engine.

60. The chassis number, inscribed on a suitably elaborate plate mounted on the scuttle.

61. Substantial quantities of sound-deadening material are used beneath the body panels, particularly the bonnet from which so much power whispers.

62. The wheel trims are of the disc easy-clean type, the only difference between Rolls-Royce and Bentley model wheels being in the emblem.

61

62

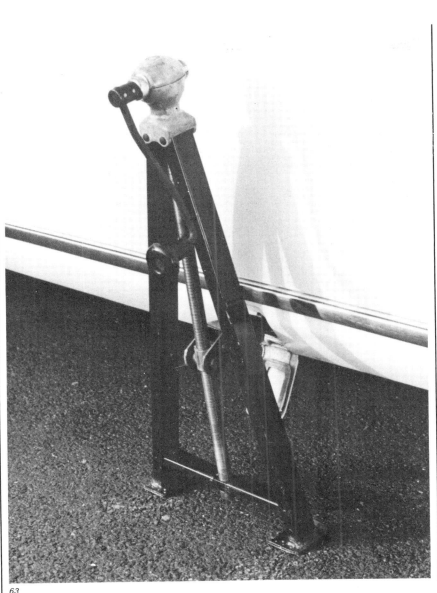

63. Even 'The Best Car in the World' is not immune to the vagaries of misfortune.

64 & 65. The suspension both front and rear is highly sophisticated and self-levelling in operation. The suspension was modified substantially in 1979 when the rear suspension destined for the new Silver Spirit was fitted. This is the early type system.

63

64

65

66

66. The rare Bentley Corniche convertible, together with the T-series saloon from which it was developed. (Copyright Rolls-Royce Motors Limited 1984).

67. A Corniche saloon. This is the intermediate model, identifiable by lack of brake air vents in the front wings, and the addition of driving lamps. (Copyright Rolls-Royce Motors Limited 1984).

67

C1

C2

C1. The Rolls-Royce Corniche has always been very much a drivers' car, as at home on a winding country lane as on the wide smooth streets of a city centre.

C2. The rear of the Corniche bears a distinct resemblance to that of the Silver Shadow, but it is individual, nonetheless, with a distinctive new wing line and, on the drop-head, the well-padded hood.

C3. It can be difficult to comprehend the sheer length of a Corniche until you see the car in profile.

C3

C4

C5

C4. When the hood is furled on a Corniche, its windows can be left erect, framed by a chromium surround.

C5. The hood, meantime, is covered with a neat tonneau of material to match the upholstery.

C6

C7

C8

C6. Not one iota does the raised hood spoil the lines of the car. The hood is a work of art in itself, taking one highly skilled man a full week's work to tailor.

C7. The early Corniche – this is a 1972 model – was fitted with elegant chromium-plated bumper bars and over-riders, with air intakes for the braking system under the headlights. The foglight and spotlight fitted above the bumper bar are optional extras.

C8. The light should always fall well on the famous Rolls-Royce radiator grille, a registered trade mark, in its position on the Corniche, tilted forward a barely-perceptible three degrees.

C9

C10

C11

C9. Air conditioned or not, there's no better way to enjoy the essence of sporting driving than with the hood furled and all the windows neatly stowed.

C10. The well-balanced lines of the Corniche are emphasised when it is viewed from the front, on high.

C11. The Spirit of Ecstacy still tops the radiator grille of the Corniche.

C12

C12. Tinted glass was a popular optional extra specified on many Corniches. The lining of their hoods was also trimmed in a colour compatible with that of the interior leather hides.

C13

C14

C13.   From early in 1977, the Corniche had to be revised to meet American safety regulations, with the most prominent change being the substitution of bumper bars of a rubberised appearance.
Copyright Rolls-Royce Motors Limited 1984

C14.   The instrument panel remained substantially the same, but some of the instruments and controls had to be re-arranged to meet the new American regulations. The steering wheel also had to adopt a padded form.